STEAM WORKS

DEREK HUNTRISS

STEAM WORKS

BCA

LONDON   NEW YORK   SYDNEY   TORONTO

Dedication:
To my wife Edith, for her patience and support through this and seven previous titles. To my sons, Christopher and Richard, for putting up with a part-time Dad.

Acknowledgements:
In addition to the enthusiastic help from the many photographers who offered their work for inclusion in this title, it could not have been produced without the cooperation of many individuals who have given the author access to well researched source material. In particular, sincere thanks must be offered to the following people:-

Bill Peto, Historical Research Officer for the Great Western Society Ltd.
W. Yeadon, who gave permission to use material from his excellent volumes of *Registers of LNER Locomotives* and who also assisted with additional material for classes of locomotives not yet covered by this series.
Richard Strange, of Steam Archive Services, for giving access to valuable source material and for correcting the validity of information from titles whose authors were not too careful in the production of some of their `facts´.
Wm. Marshall Shaw, Hon Group Secretary of the North British Railway Study Group, whose material is presented in the chapter relating to Cowlairs Works.
R.Jackson, Membership Secretary of the Great North of Scotland Railway Association, for information used in the chapter relating to Inverurie Works.
T.B. McGhie, Archivist of the Caledonian Railway Association, for information used in the chapter relating to St Rollox Works.
John Cordingley, Sales Officer of the Great Eastern Railway Society, for information used in the chapter relating to Stratford Works.

Bibliography:
BREL: *Swindon Works* ; BREL
Rex Christiansen: *Rail Centres - Crewe;* Ian Allan
Paul Collins: *Rail Centres - Wolverhampton;* Ian Allan
B.K. Cooper: *Rail Centres - Brighton;* Ian Allan
G.E.R.S.: Reprint - *Memoranda Connected with the Locomotive and Carriage Works at Stratford and the Wagon Works at Temple Mills;* Passmore Edwards Museum & the Great Eastern Railway Society
G.N.S.R. Association: Reprint - *LNER Inverurie Locomotive Carriage & Wagon Works;* G.N.S.R. Association
Edgar Larkin: *An Illustrated History of British Railways´ Workshops;* OPC
E.R. Mountford: *Caerphilly Works 1901-1964;* Roundhouse Books
A.D. Nugent: *A Short History of Stratford Major Depot;* G.E.R.S.
J.B. Radford: *Derby Works and Midland Locomotives;* Ian Allan
Southern Railway: *Ashford Works Centenary 1847-1947;* The Baynard Press
Susan Jane Woods & Peter Tuffery: *Doncaster Plant Works;* Bond Publications
W.B. Yeadon: *Yeadon´s Register of LNER Locomotives Vols 1-5;* Irwell Press
Other Publications: *Backtrack, British Railway Journal, British Railways Illustrated, Modern Railways, Railway Magazine, Railway World, Steam Days, Steam Railway, Steam World, Trains Illustrated, The World of Trains.*

Derek Huntriss   Camborne
                                                      Cornwall
                                                      May 1994

Half-title page:
`Castle´ class 4-6-0 No 5045 *Earl of Dudley* stands outside Swindon Works on 16 February 1958 prior to re-entering traffic at its home depot at Wolverhampton Stafford Road (84A). No 5045 had received a Heavy General repair and at this date had completed some 1,190,996 miles in traffic. The nameplate was formerly carried by an `Earl´ class 4-4-0, its slight misfitting on the curved splasher being visible. *W.Potter*

Title page:
The pioneer of the last series of the class, `King Arthur´ class 4-6-0 No 30793 *Sir Ontzlake*, is depicted at Eastleigh MPD on 25 August 1957 having just emerged from a General repair. This series of the class had the 6-wheeled 3,500 gallon tenders for use on the Brighton section, although No 30793 ran with an eight-wheeled tender between 1959 and 1962 when it was withdrawn. *R.C. Riley*

Front Cover:
Following a full repaint at Darlington Works, Class Q7 0-8-0 No 63460 heads the RCTS/SLS 'North Eastern Tour' south of Broncepeth on 28 September 1963. Fortunately, No 63460 has been secured for preservation and currently operates on the North Yorkshire Moors Railway. *T. B. Owen*

Rear cover top:
A view inside Eastleigh Works with a tank engine pictured on the rollers. *T. B. Owen*

Rear cover middle:
'Britannia' Pacific No 70021 *Morning Star* moves slowly up the yard at Willesden (1A) MPD on 9 October 1963. At this date, Willesden was home to no fewer than 14 'Britannias', six of these having been transferred from March (31B) MPD where they had been displaced by English Electric Type 3 diesels. *G. Rixon*

Rear cover bottom:
Following an intermediate repair during which it had been fitted with ATC equipment, Stanier 2-6-4T No 42489 stands outside Crewe Works on 19 February 1961. Having arrived at works on 28 January, No 42489 was to return to its home depot at Bangor (6H). *A. N. H. Glover*

CONTENTS

Fresh from overhaul at Cowlairs Works, Derby-designed `Clan' No 72009 *Clan Stewart* is depicted at Carlisle Kingmoor (12A) MPD in September 1962. The 1952 built, Derby-designed `Clans' were intended to replace pre-Grouping locos in Scotland. Unexpectedly heavy coal consumption led to the curtailment of the programme, only 10 engines being built *G. Rixon*

INTRODUCTION

As a time-served Precision Engineer heavily involved with the introduction of computer-aided manufacturing techniques over the last 30 years, I have always had a healthy respect for my forebears, particularly those in the field of locomotive construction who managed to produce such handsome and effective machines with what would be described today as primitive technologies. With the exception of the earliest years of the railways, when newly formed companies relied heavily on private contractors to construct their locomotives, the railway companies of Britain designed and built a large percentage of their own locomotives in addition to carrying out regular repair work. It was the continuation of these practices that led to the construction of a wide range of classes, each with their own distinctive differences in design and appearance.

For the first time in colour, this title portrays many different classes as they were seen in `Ex-Works´ condition on British Railways in the 1950s and 1960s. In addition to these there are many pictures taken inside the locomotive workshops as well as those depicting locomotives operating at the major workshops as pilots or shunters. To add depth to the background of the development of the various types of motive power that survived into this period, there is an outline history of each of the workshops in this title. Whilst all of the major locomotive workshops are included, some of the smaller operations have been covered where colour photographic material was available.

From December 1948, authorisation of locomotive construction programmes lay with each Chief Mechanical Engineer and the authority given by him formed the basis of the Works procedure. Whilst there was a Production Planning Organisation at the main works of the former LMS railway, at the works of other railways, these functions were delegated to the Shop supervisory staff or to separate sections of the Works Manager´s organisation.

The methods of progressing locomotive engine repairs through the workshops varied considerably and broadly speaking the methods governing a locomotives´s entry into the Works were comparable, the differences which existed stemming largely from geographical considerations. Independent examinations of locomotives which determined the degree of repair work necessary were developed only by the former GWR and LMS companies where repairs required were determined by the appropriate Shop Foreman and Chargehands. The use of time schedules to control the repair work was universal, although on the workshops of the former Southern Railway, this applied only to General Repairs.

Where possible, details of repairs being carried out to locomotives illustrated in this title have been given. In order to add meaning to these descriptions, the following list of Classified Repairs as applied to locomotives on the LNER was taken from *Yeadon´s Register of LNER Locomotives - Vol 1 - Gresley A1 and A3 Classes.*

`Heavy Repairs´ :
(a) Engines re-boilered.
(b) Boiler taken out of frame for general repair.
(c) New tyres fitted to four or more wheels.
(d) Fitting new cylinders.
(e) Fitting new axles, engine or tender.
(f) Retubing.
(g) Turning up wheels and re-fitting boxes; or motion and brakework stripped and overhauled.
(h) Boiler repairs in frame with not less than 50 stays renewed.

`Light Repairs´ :
(a) Fitting new axle or axles, engine or tender.
(b) Taking out and replace 50 or more boiler tubes.
(c) Taking out and replace four or more superheater flue tubes.
(d) Taking down and replacing superheater header.
(e) Renewal of piston valve liners or piston valves.
(f) Fitting new tyres to one or more wheels.
(g) Turning up four or more wheels and re-fitting boxes.
(h) Complete overhaul of one or more valve gears.
(i) Fitting patch on boiler or fire box.
(j) Renewing 30 or more firebox stays.
(k) Fitting four or more new axleboxes, or engine axlebox brasses.
(l) Welding, patching, or straightening frame, or renewing buffer beam.
(m) Re-boring cylinders and re-facing ports.
(n) Taking off and repairing tanks.

Other Repairs: Those which necessitated the engine being out of traffic for 24 hours or over ending midnight and not coming under `Heavy´ or `Light´.

Operations at the workshops covered in this title continued largely unchecked until 1954 when the government approved BR´s £1,600 million `Reorganisation Plan´. Whilst these changes improved operations at BR workshops, the levels of staff required to keep them operational was mainly unaltered until the drastic proposals for the British Transport Commission´s workshops closures were announced in 1962. With the demise of the steam locomotive with its inherently high maintenance requirements, it was estimated that the total amount of work would drop by one third over the succeeding five years. At that time average use was only 80% of capacity, a figure which was calculated to drop to 55% in 1966. The proposals were that 12 of the 29 main workshops would be closed over the next three years, the total number of employees dropping from 56,000 to 38,000. Contrasting factors were the difficulty which some discharged older men might have in obtaining skilled work - in boiler repairs, for instance - and the effect of normal wastage in minimising redundancies. The estimated savings of these proposals were about £30 million per year on the then cost of £100 million. However, these plans had to be revised, in part, due to the hostile reaction from the trade unions.

By the end of the 1960s, BR´s own major design work was concentrated at the Railway Technical Centre at Derby, a practice that was continued until the 1980s when the Railway divested itself of new design activity. One of the most notable achievements of the period was the development of the High Speed Train. Designed for running at 125 mph, these trains soon transformed the speed and standard of services on non-electrified routes. Other major design projects were the updating of the Class 87 electric locomotive´s design for further construction as Class 90.

Today, with the recent privatisation of the remaining major railway workshops, the fascinating story of locomotive, carriage and wagon construction has come to an end.

It is hoped, that readers will be able to recall their favourite locomotive types, seen here resplendent in `Ex-Works´ condition before a few weeks of operation in traffic transformed their appearance.

Top:
Photographed outside Swindon Works in May 1963, former GWR `Prairie´ 2-6-2T No 8109 has been outshopped with the route colour code under the cabside numberplate, a feature usually applied above the numberplate. *D. Penney*

Above:
Built in September 1872 as No 72 *Fenchurch* and pictured as BR No 32636 outside Eastleigh MPD on 23 April 1962, this locomotive survives today on the Bluebell Railway and holds the distinction of being the oldest, continually working loco in Britain. *G.W. Morrison*

HR `Jones Goods´ 4-6-0 No 103 heads an RCTS/SLS railtour at Slochd, between Aviemore and Inverness on 15 June 1960. Built by Sharp Stewart and Co in 1894, the 15 members of the class were the first examples of the 4-6-0 in the British Isles. *T.B. Owen*

Above:
Fresh from the Paint Shop at Crewe Works, No 46250 *City of Lichfield* emerges from the south end of Kilsby Tunnel with the 12 noon Liverpool to Euston service on 6 June 1962. Unfortunately, a preservation attempt by Lichfield Town Council was unsuccessful. *Peter Fitton*

Ex-Works McIntosh Caledonian 0-4-4T No 55220 stands out from the crowd at Polmadie (66A) MPD on 25 May 1958. Introduced by the Caledonian Railway in 1900 as 'Standard Passenger' Class, one member, BR No 55189, survives in preservation as CR 419 at Bo'ness. *P.W.Gray*

Photographed at Carnforth (10A) MPD during the last week of BR steam operations in August 1968, Britannia Pacific No 70013 *Oliver Cromwell* has the distinction of being the last BR steam locomotive to be overhauled in normal service. This last Ex-Works locomotive was the centre-piece of a ceremony marking the event at Crewe Works on 2 February 1967. For the event No 70013 carried its original nameplates. *Derek Huntriss*

Smartly lined-out following a General Repair, No 7824 *Iford Manor* is seen outside Swindon (82C) MPD on 4 May 1958 prior to returning to its home depot at Carmarthen (87G). No 7824 had been transferred to Carmarthen from Penzance (83G) MPD in July 1957. *T.B. Owen*

ONE

SWINDON

Having received the Royal Assent, parliament sanctioned the Great Western Railway Act in August 1835 for the construction of a railway between London and Bristol. The young Isambard Kingdom Brunel was appointed as Engineer to the company and three months later, the first section of broad gauge (7ft) from Paddington to Maidenhead Riverside was opened. By December 1840 the line had been extended through Swindon and by June 1841 was completely opened through to Bristol. Brunel appointed the young Daniel Gooch as Superintendent of locomotives, a position he was to hold for the next 27 years.

Locomotives ordered by the company from independent suppliers were far from satisfactory and caused the young Locomotive Superintendent considerable trouble. The rapid growth of the railway necessitated the provision of a central repair depot and Mr Gooch was asked to determine a suitable site. In his report he favoured Swindon as the location, basing his recommendation on purely technical grounds. Gradients on the line were favourable and the junction with the line to Cheltenham was also at a spot where the canal afforded a direct connection with the Somerset coalfield. This recommendation was approved by the Directors and the construction was authorised on 25 February 1841. It is interesting to note that much of the stone used for construction came from excavations made in pushing the new line through Box Hill.

By November 1842 the machinery had been started although the Works were not fully operational until January 1843 and at that time employed over 400 men. Impressed by the success of the Great Western Railway, competitors operating narrow gauge (4ft 8$\frac{1}{2}$in) railways were spurred on to construct more powerful locomotives. Mindful of this the Great Western built their first passenger locomotive, *Great Western* - "a colossal locomotive working with all speed". This locomotive, built with an all out effort at Swindon, was completed in 13 weeks and was first steamed on 1 April 1846. Such was its success, an order for a further six engines of similar design was placed. Also in 1846, the death knell for the ambitious broad gauge was sounded by the Gauge Commissioners who favoured the now standard 4ft 8$\frac{1}{2}$in.

After several amalgamations with other smaller railways, it became obvious to the directors that vast amounts of rolling stock, both broad and standard gauge, had been acquired, and that there was a need for a central complex for the construction and maintenance of carriages and wagons. After the consideration of Oxford for the site of these works, Swindon was once again chosen, the construction commencing in June 1868 and the first coaching stock constructed entering traffic in late 1869. At this time it was realised that the mixing of broad and narrow gauge operations caused many problems and it was decided to commence a gradual conversion to standard gauge. Thirteen miles of extra sidings were laid down at Swindon for the fleets of locomotives and rolling stock to be converted to standard gauge or broken up. Of the 195 locomotives involved, 130 engines had been built so as to be readily convertible as had a large proportion of the Carriage & Wagon stock.

Locomotive design at Swindon had undergone little change since the days of Gooch, Armstrong & Dean until the arrival of G.J. Churchward, who became Assistant Chief Superintendent in 1897 and who took full responsibility from 1902. The locomotives built by Churchward could not be built by orthodox methods and a constant stream of new sheds, lifting tackle, heavy presses and traversing bays had to be ordered. In the decade following 1900, all extensions with a few exceptions were all

in the carriage works. These were good times for the shareholders, as dividends did not drop below 5% and reached 6% in 1913. The number of passengers carried, 50 million in 1885, rose steadily until it reached 80 million by 1900 and topped 100 million in 1908.

One of the most important introductions came in 1902 with the construction of the 4-6-0 passenger locomotive No 100 *William Dean*, the prototype for GWR passenger locomotives for the next 50 years. Only five years later, the 4-cylinder `Star´ class made its debut and on the passenger carrying side the 70ft `Dreadnought´ was introduced in 1904, these giving an increase in passenger accommodation. About this time the predecessor of today´s DMUs arrived in the form of the steam-rail motor set. In 1907 the Works Gas Works were increased in area and in 1908 the motive power depot was doubled in size. In addition to these facilities, subways were constructed to facilitate access from the works.

The year 1908 saw the construction of the first `Pacific´ locomotive No 111 *The Great Bear* - the first 4-6-2 in Britain. The period of World War 1 restricted expansion considerably, plans for completing the second half of `A´ shop being shelved until 1919. During the war, much production was turned over to the manufacture of armaments, which included various types of heavy howitzers together with 60 pounder Hotchkiss and A.A. guns. In addition to large quantities of miscellaneous equipment, the works also produced large quantities of medium and heavy calibre shells. Locomotives of the `Dean Goods´ class were constructed for War Department use overseas, both in France and the Middle East. Many of these never returned.

By the early 1920s the Works had swallowed up all the land purchased and further expansion on that site was prevented. A new Carriage Stock Shed was built on what was a part of a Corporation playing field. This was acquired by handing over the GWR park in 1928. From then on only comparatively small alterations took place, but 1923 had seen the debut of the first `Castle´ class Locomotive No 4073 *Caerphilly Castle*. This engine was to feature in the British Empire Exhibition of 1924/1925.

By 1925 Swindon Works employed some 14,000 people and the year 1927 saw the introduction of the first `King´ class 4-6-0 *King George V*, in honour of the sovereign. This was the most powerful locomotive built at Swindon to date and was to represent this country at the Baltimore and Ohio Railways Fair of the Iron Horse in Baltimore, Maryland, USA. The following year, 1928, saw the appearance of the `Hall´ class locomotive, a down to earth workhorse which was later constructed in large numbers. In the 1930s the works were at their largest in land area - some 326 acres, and only relatively small additions and developments were made.

The austerity of the World War 2 years saw changes of little note, the works once again being called upon to produce many items of war equipment including gun mountings, landing craft and midget submarine superstructures. The `Dean Goods´ 0-6-0s were once again converted for war use in addition to a large number of Stanier 2-8-0s which were produced for both the United Kingdom and for use abroad, particularly the Persian Gulf.

Prior to the formation of the British Transport Commission in 1948, the year 1945 saw the introduction of the `County´ class locomotive and on 15 November 1950 the works were visited by HRH Princess Elizabeth who formally named the last member of the `Castle´ class to be constructed, No 7037 *Swindon*. The 1950s became the decade of Standard class locomotive construction, many types being designed and built up until 1960. This year saw the construction of the last steam locomotive for BR, a `9F´ 2-10-0 No 92220 *Evening Star*. Overlapping this period was the commencement of dieselisation, the first diesel-hydraulic `Warship´ class No D800 *Sir Brian Robertson* being completed in July 1958. The first three members of this class were a belated addition to BR´s pilot scheme orders; and whilst the design was almost entirely due to German engineering skill, No D800 was constructed almost entirely by hand, the staff at Swindon having to translate specifications into a design that would fit the British loading gauge.

The Main Workshops Future Plan of 1962 called for the closure of 15 workshops out of a total of 31. At Swindon all new building work was transferred to other shops with the exception of BRUTE trolleys used for handling parcels. At this time the Carriage and Wagon Works were closed and the old Locomotive Works were reconditioned and modified to undertake the repair work to carriages and wagons in addition to loco-

motives. In 1962, a new Diesel Testing station was completed, this being built on the site of the old Stripping Shed. At this time when many older buildings were being demolished or reconditioned, a new Apprentice Training School was opened as well as a new Dining Hall and Medical Centre.

With the phased withdrawal of the diesel-hydraulics in the early 1970s, a further reduction of the workforce was necessitated. On 1 January 1970, the works became part of British Rail Engineering Ltd and in September 1973, the last diesel-hydraulic locomotive to receive a classified repair - Class 52 No D1029 *Western Legionnaire* - returned to traffic. Also during this period there was was the large scale scrapping of diesel locomotives, although in 1976, the preserved Stanier Pacific No 46229 *Duchess of Hamilton* paid a visit for overhaul.Although the works had commenced refurbishment of Southern Region EMUs and they had also constructed 20 metre-gauge locomotives for Kenya Railways, it was in 1985 that complete closure of the works was announced. Following this the works was sold to Tarmac Swindon Ltd in 1987 who redeveloped part of the site into a community called Churchward.

Photographed outside Swindon Works on 7 February 1960, double-chimneyed, No 1000 *County of Middlesex* , carries the white X above the numberplate denoting that it is able to haul trains in excess of the permitted limit for the class. *T.B. Owen*

No 6025 *King Henry III* takes water from Goring troughs as it heads a two coach running-in turn on 16 January 1954. No 6025 was later to return to Laira (83D) MPD following its Heavy Intermediate repair. *T.B. Owen*

Top:
`9400´ class 0-6-0PT No 8481 catches the spring sunshine outside Swindon Works in April 1963. No 8481 had entered the Works for a General repair on 11 March and was returned to Old Oak Common (81A) MPD when completed. *D. Penney*

Bottom:
2-6-2T No 6163 is depicted at Swindon following a Heavy General repair on 4 November 1962. This class had higher boiler pressure for faster acceleration on suburban services out of Paddington in an effort to overcome competition from motor transport. *A.N.H. Glover*

Above:
Southall-based 4-6-0 No 4934 *Hindlip Hall* is depicted at Old Oak Common (81A) MPD on 29 August 1959 following a Heavy General repair at Swindon. Today, Hindlip Hall is better known as the Worcestershire Police Headquarters. *R.C. Riley*

Below:
Cardiff Cathays (88A) based `9F´ 2-10-0 No 92208 seen outside Swindon Works on 17 June 1962. During the course of 1965 the Western Region withdrew its entire allocation of the class including some locomotives which had been built little more than five years earlier. *W. Potter*

Left:

A Preservationist's Dream - lines of ready-made smokeboxes for many different types of locomotive - all off the shelf. This collection of parts for use in future repairs was photographed outside the Works at Swindon on 26 March 1961. *T.B. Owen*

Left:

Today, worth a small fortune as collectors´ items, this selection of copper-capped chimneys were merely locomotive spares worth little more than the cost of the material used when seen outside Swindon works on 24 March 1963. *T.B. Owen*

Below:

Fitted with a Hawksworth straight-sided tender, `Modified Hall´ No 7900 *Saint Peter's Hall* **heads an up fitted parcels train near Twyford on 19 April 1958. This loco is a credit to the shed staff at Oxford who have kept her in Ex-Works condition since her last Heavy Intermediate repair at Swindon, completed on 5 December 1957.**

T.B. Owen

Pictured inside the vast 'A' shop at Swindon on 27 January 1963, Swansea East Dock's (87D) 0-6-2T No 6602 has received a Heavy General repair. Unusually the safety valve bonnet has been painted over - something that would not have occurred in earlier years. *T.B. Owen*

An excellent portrait of an impressive locomotive. Allocated to Aberdare (86J) MPD, 2-8-0T No 4257 had received a Heavy General repair when it was photographed outside Swindon Works on 7 February 1960. This class of locomotives was mainly used for heavy mineral traffic in South Wales. *T.B. Owen*

4257

4-4-0 No 3717 *City of Truro* **is seen in Swindon Works `A´ shop on 18 March 1960 following a repaint before leaving for exhibition. It should be noted that the locomotive's handrails have been polished, a practice which was common to all GWR locomotives up until 1916. Before that date, when the practice was discontinued due to the pressures of World War 1, they would be cleaned by the fireman at the end of each trip. After 1916, the only locomotives to receive this treatment were the `Kings´ and locomotives posing for official photographs.** *W. Potter*

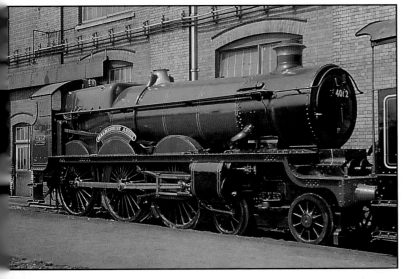

Left:
Former GWR `Star´ class 4-6-0 No 4062 *Malmesbury Abbey* **has been beautifully lined out following a Heavy Intermediate repair. Allocated to Swindon (82C) MPD, No 4062 is depicted outside the Works on 27 April 1952.** *T.B. Owen*

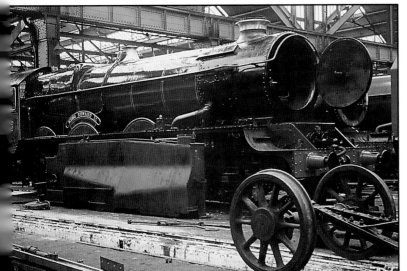

Left:
Prior to returning to Laira (83D) MPD, blue-liveried No 6023 *King Edward II* **is seen undergoing a Heavy General repair inside Swindon Works `A´ shop on 2 March 1952. Still surviving today, No 6023 is being restored at the Great Western Society's depot at Didcot where it will be fitted with a single chimney.** *T.B. Owen*

21

Right:
Only six days after leaving Swindon where it had undergone a Heavy General repair, Tyseley's '4300' 2-6-0 No 7317 is at Oxford on 5 September 1960 having arrived with a train from Birmingham, its headlamp code was incorrect for a light engine. *G.W. Morrison*

Above:
Former GWR heavy freight 2-8-0 No 2895 is depicted near Maidenhead with a loose-coupled through freight in September 1962. Outshopped from Swindon after a Heavy General repair on 30 August, No 2895, allocated to Severn Tunnel Junction (86E) MPD, was one of a batch of 16 locos introduced in 1938 which were fitted with side-window cabs. *D. Penney*

Left:
Photographed at Didcot on 25 July 1963, `Prairie´ 2-6-2T No 6136 appears to have had its safety valve bonnet painted over during its recent visit to Swindon Works where it had undergone Heavy General repair. *K. Fairey*

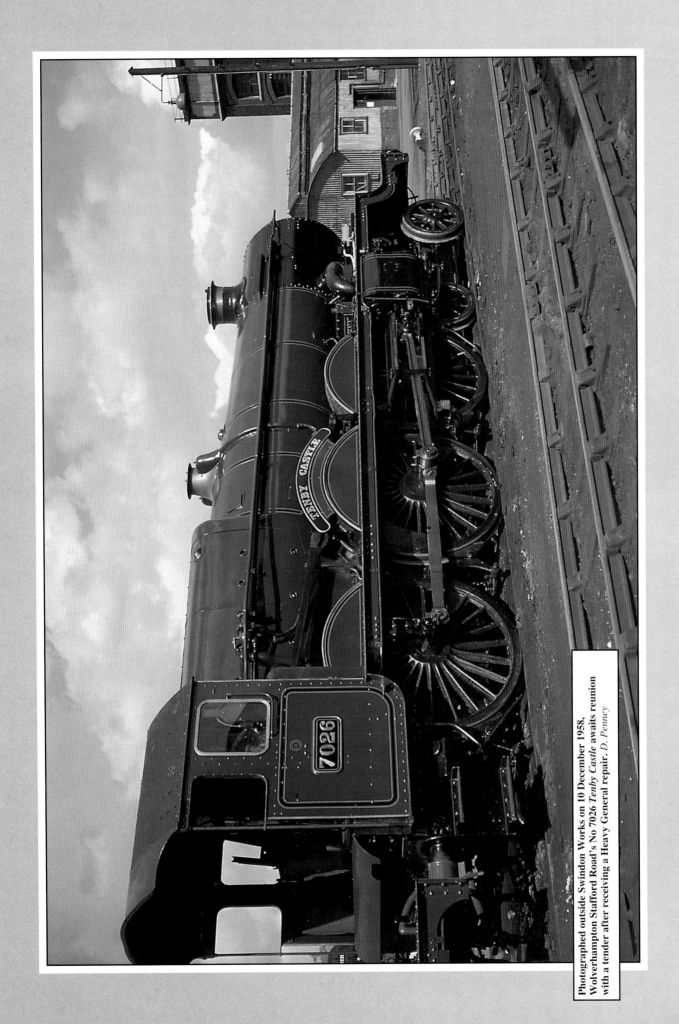

Photographed outside Swindon Works on 10 December 1958, Wolverhampton Stafford Road's No 7026 *Tenby Castle* awaits reunion with a tender after receiving a Heavy General repair. *D. Penney*

Top:
No 4074 *Caldicot Castle* **has yet to receive a chimney as she undergoes a Heavy Intermediate repair at Swindon on 1 April 1959. Also to be fitted with a front bogie and undergo a full repaint, No 4074 was returned to her home depot at Landore (87E) on 15 April.** *T.B. Owen*

Above:
No 1011 *County of Chester* **is seen outside Swindon Works on 4 November 1962 and awaits return to St Philip's Marsh (82B) MPD. Locomotive water at that depot came from the River Avon and footplate staff often found fish and eels in locomotive tenders.** *A.N.H. Glover*

Above:
Built by the GWR in February 1907, No 4003 *Lode Star* was withdrawn from traffic on 18 July 1951 after completing some 2,005,898 miles in revenue earning service, the seventh highest total of any GWR locomotive. Pictured inside Swindon Works on 29 April 1962, No 4003 has had its smokebox interior painted white for exhibition purposes. *T.B. Owen*

Below:
Two weeks later, final painting completed, No 4003 is being manoeuvred into position on a Pickford's low loader prior to permanent retirement inside Swindon Museum. *T.B. Owen*

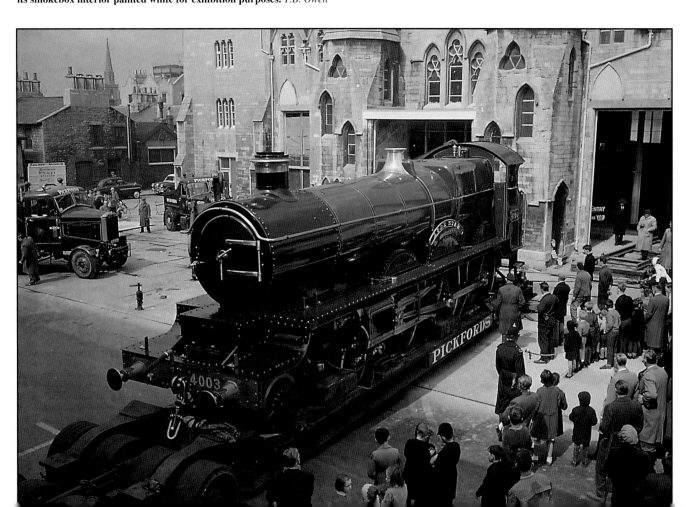

Above:
Officially the last locomotive to receive a repair at Newton Abbot, 2-6-2T No 4566 leaves the factory on 15 July 1960. Repainted after her Light Casual repair, No 4566 worked on running-in turns around Newton Abbot for about a week before despatch to Penzance MPD. *P.W. Gray*

Below:
One week later, No 4566 was photographed at Truro, presumably *en route* to Penzance. An escapee from Barry scrap-yard, No 4566 has now enjoyed many years of preservation and can be seen in traffic on the Severn Valley Railway. *R.C. Riley*

TWO

NEWTON ABBOT

Shortly after reaching Newton Abbot at the end of 1846, the broad gauge South Devon Railway constructed a small two road shed. By 1851 the South Devon maintained only three depots, the arrangements at Newton being described as 'One Engine Shed and Engine Men´s Room constructed with Wood, the former used for lighting and cleaning engines and supplied with Gas and Water, with two lines of rails; one Large Repairing Shop constructed with Wood on Stone foundations; one Smiths´ Shop built with Timber fitted with six Hearths and Bellows; one Store Room built with Timber; one Boilerhouse with high Chimney attached built of stone; one Shafting and Drums in Repairing Shop; one nine inch self acting Lathe; one 12 inch self acting Lathe; one ten inch Lathe for Wood Turning; one Planing Machine with Table 5ft 6in by 2ft 2is; one Small Punching and Shearing Machine; one Vertical Drilling Machine; one Grindstone with Cast Iron Trough; 14 Vices; 4 Anvils; one Horse Pump with Pipes complete; one Water Tank made of Wood; one 34ft Wooden Turntable; two Water Cranes with Pipes to the Tanks'.

The end of the broad gauge in May 1892 brought about a complete reordering of matters on the South Devon and at Newton Abbot locomotive servicing arrangements were improved with the construction of a new engine shed and workshops. Built from local stone the works closely followed the outline of its predecessor in that it comprised a number of locomotive bays accessed by a traverser running the length of the main building. Examination of various plans shows that the new building was erected to the north of the old one, leaving room for the improved engine shed.

The factory at Newton Abbot was fashioned by the GWR in line with their practices at Swindon where one of the bays had two points of entry served by a covered traverser. Wholly separated from the locomotive running shed, the barriers and boundaries were rarely, if ever, crossed. The practice of moving a locomotive from the turntable on to the traverser was assigned to men from the shed and after that it was up to the employees from the Works. Outside the Works in the yard, locomotives and tenders were separated and hauled off turntables by hawser and capstan. On both sides of the traverser there were separate gangs of fitters who were served by overhead cranes, each gang being under the authority of a Chargeman Fitter, who, wearing immaculate overalls, had godlike powers. It was only the boiler smiths´ gang that were to be found working in all parts of the factory. As at many railway establishments of its day there were regular minor injuries such as burns, cuts, grazes, crushed fingers and the like. It would have been a nightmare for any present day safety officers. Outside the Works against the west wall was a peculiar operation known as the Bosh House where brake hangers and other parts from working steam locomotives were boiled in caustic soda and steam to remove years of oil and grime. The worst accident occurring at Newton was that when an unfortunate individual was killed when he fell into this contraption.

Not all roads inside the Works were of equal length. The only way to get a `King´ into the shops was from the smaller Works turntable which would just take a `King´ without its tender. All equipment inside the Factory, with the exception of a wheel lathe, was belt-driven, power being generated by two stationary boilers, one in use, one spare. An ancient broad gauge engine was set up on bricks and connected to spindles which in turn powered the drive belts. Electric welding equipment was installed in 1939 to cope with the high incidence of collision damage work on bent buffer beams. Tanks from '55XX' locomotives were often found on the outside roads of the traverser while work on the rest of the locomotive continued inside. In the days before knowledge of the effects of asbestos dust, clouds would billow across as a boiler was stripped down, after which it was recycled with new material being added in a great tub of water and was then plastered back on with a float.

The Subsidiary Works of the Great Western Railway were those defined as establishments which carried out classified but not General repairs. By reason of their even geographical distribution throughout the system the subsidiary workshops were used to save light mileage in working engines for the lighter classified repairs in the Main Works at Swindon, Wolverhampton and Caerphilly. These Subsidiary Works were also used as convenient centres for the upkeep of outdoor machinery within the division. In fact this latter mentioned work was often of greater volume than locomotive repairs, staff used on either duty according to the work available. Under the control of Divisional Superintendents, who also controlled the Running Sheds, the Subsidiary Works were also available to relieve the Running Sheds of Unclassified repairs if capacity was available.

Figures collated by the GWR in 1947 show that at any one time there was an average of 14.1 locomotives under repair and in the course of the year the works undertook a total of 195 Light repairs. These figures, together with those from other Subsidiary Works, endorsed the fact that their usefulness was dependent upon their ability to undertake Light Classified repairs with speed and to save time and mileage which locomotives would have taken in order to reach the Main Works. This capacity also relieved pit space at the Main Works for Heavy repairs. Whether the Subsidiary Works were economic concerns was a question of policy and equipment rather than of organisation.

An expensive Division in terms of locomotive coal, the postwar solution of oil fuelling being considered for Newton Abbot. Diesel motive power was considered at an early stage and at one time a scheme to carry out electrification in the west had been proposed. The boiler house, pump house and tanks were erected beyond the exit road more or less on the site of the old broad gauge shed. This installation saw little proper use, but as at many sites, it came into its own for diesel cars, two new 7,000 gallon tanks being proposed in 1957 and three fuelling roads were ordered for DMU sets. The advent of diesel motive power saw the end of steam repairs at Newton Abbot, the last locomotive to receive a Classified repair being 2-6-2T No 4566 which was driven out of the Works by the Lord Mayor (see picture opposite). The old factory closed in July 1960, work then beginning on remodelling it for diesel maintenance. By March 1962, the steam age had been obliterated completely, the factory being altered with the removal of the traverser to the outside, at right angles to its former position. This advent of quietly humming new technology was a major contrast to the days of steam operations, and astonishingly was swept away in its turn, the remaining building of both Running Shed and Works being scheduled for demolition later this year, 1994.

Right:
2-8-2T No 7203 is seen outside Caerphilly Works before returning to Aberdare (86J) MPD after receiving a Heavy Intermediate repair in September 1960. Built as 2-8-2T No 5278 in September 1930, she was placed in immediate store due to the collapse of the coal industry. Stored at Swindon, she was altered to 2-8-2T No 7203 at a cost of £200.00 and dispatched to Newport MPD on 20 September 1934.
T.A. Murphy/Colour-Rail

Above:
Only one week after leaving Caerphilly factory after a Heavy General repair, Llanelly (87F) based 2-6-0 No 6389 heads an up ecs working near Starcross on 13 July 1957. Not visible in this view is the red reversing lever, a trade mark of Caerphilly which was applied to all tender engines passing through shops. *P.W. Gray*

Left:
GWR 0-6-2T No 5689 is seen at Cardiff Canton (86C) MPD on 4 September 1960. No 5689 had undergone a Heavy Intermediate repair at Caerphilly between 20 June and 26 August 1960 and was presumably at Canton on a running-in turn prior to its return to Westbury (82D) MPD. *P.W. Gray*

28

THREE

CAERPHILLY

Sited on the eastern borders of the town, the railway workshops at Caerphilly were opened by the Rhymney Railway in 1901. Principally known locally as `The Sheds´, the buildings at Caerphilly Works were sufficiently completed for an inspection by the directors on 20 July 1900, although it was not until December 1901 that they were finally in operation. Built in two widely separated sections, at the east end of the site being that for the locomotive shops and the west end for carriage and wagon. The locomotive Works consisted of one main building 245ft 0in long which was divided into seven bays forming six individual workshops. Starting from the northern end these were as follows:

Machine Shop. One 42ft wide bay equipped with several heavy duty lathes including wheel and crank machines in addition to many more general purpose machine tools.

Erecting Shop. Two bays, totalling 86ft 0in wide, each bay having two rail tracks with engine pits. Each track was capable of stabling five engines, although in normal practice, only four per road were normally under repair.

Test Shop. One bay 35ft 0in wide where a variety of work including Westinghouse brake test and locomotive weighing took place. One rail track led into this shop from the Works yard on which the Works and Goods yard pilots were stabled and lit up each morning.

Smiths´ Shop. One 42ft wide bay equipped with a 12cwt steam hammer, a large spring furnace, fourteen smiths´ hearths and the usual run of anvils, surface plates and swage blocks.

Boiler Test Shop. One bay 35ft wide of which only one part was used for testing boilers, the remainder being used as a steel stores and for a short time as a toolroom.

Boiler Shop. One 42ft wide bay with a 10-ton capacity electric overhead gantry crane. Plant included large and small plate rolls, punching and shearing machine, radial driller, machine saw and tool grinder.

The Works at Caerphilly had replaced the Rhymney Railways´ original workshops which were situated at Cardiff Docks. The only main railway workshops in South Wales, it served the 23-mile stretch of line from Rhymney to Cardiff. Although the Works did not actually construct locomotives, it undertook a large amount of repair work and also undertook the standardising and modernisation of existing locomotives. Before 1922 the Works undertook work only on Rhymney Railway locomotives, but after this time work was carried out for other railway companies, the site at Caerphilly being considerably expanded. At about that time the number of employees peaked at around 700 and after 1923 it became part of the Great Western Railway.

The amalgamation of the railways forming the Western group took place in stages, constituent companies being dealt with first, the smaller absorbed companies being dealt with later. It would be difficult to establish an actual date when the GWR took full working control, although in the case of the Rhymney Railway this was on 25 March 1922, and, as with other companies, financial transactions were backdated to 1 January. Until August 1922 the Works at Caerphilly had dealt solely with Rhymney Railway locomotives, and on the 5th of that month, instructions were issued to the effect that henceforth engines passing through the factory were to be painted in GWR colours and renumbered. At that time GW numberplates were not available for all engines and in several cases the Rhymney number and RR initials were painted out and the GW

number painted on in lieu, a piecework price of one penny a number or letter being allowed. Engines of the former Barry and Cardiff Railways began to arrive for repair at this time, the first Barry Railway locos being 0-6-2Ts, Class B No 23 and Class B1 No 116 which appeared on 7 September.

The most important change at Caerphilly in the postwar period was the nationalisation of the railways as from 1 January 1948. Initially the change had little impact at Caerphilly excepting the fact that the world famous initials GWR were passing into history after a period of over 110 years. On 2 February 1948, instructions were given that the words `BRITISH RAILWAYS´ should replace the GWR initials on engines passing through shops for repair, the letters to be 5 in high. At the same time instructions were given that the letter W, denoting Western Region, was to be painted below the moulding of GWR numberplates, this letter having to be 3in high with a space of ¹/₂in between the bottom rim of the plate and the top of the letter. Also at this time it was stated that in due course cast iron smokebox numberplates would be available, to replace the engine numbers that were painted on the front buffer beam. The next decorative change came in late 1949 when the first British Railways coat of arms were available. These came in two sizes, initially with a 16 in diameter circle, the first loco at Caerphilly to receive this being 0-6-2T No 5682 on 18 October, followed by a larger version with 28in diameter circle, the first engines to receive these being 2-8-0T No 4255 and 0-6-2T No 5649 on 8 December.

Another directive from 1 January 1949 concerned a new system of classification for locomotive repairs. Heavy repairs were divided into three categories: Heavy General (H/G), Heavy Intermediate (H/I) and Heavy Casual (H/C). The main difference between H/G and H/I was the extent of the repair carried out to the boiler being re-fitted, not to the boiler being removed, both categories covering the complete overhaul of engine components. Light repairs were classified in two sub-divisions, Light Intermediate (L/I) and Light Casual (L/C). In practice the L/I was a classification rarely used at Caerphilly and the category formerly known as Running repairs was renamed Unclassified (UN).

During 1955 the dislocation caused by the ASLEF strike was felt at the works, as it was throughout the rest of the country. Starting at midnight on Saturday 28 May, it meant that no movement of engines to or from the factory was possible for the duration of the strike. Neither was it possible for the Enparts Van, which brought certain repaired articles and spare components from Swindon, to visit the yard. Also curtailed at this time was the works train bringing employees to the factory, although for the first few days a spasmodic service was maintained in the Cardiff Valleys, the bulk of the staff managing to get to work at a reasonable time. By 5 June these passenger services were totally suspended and were not resumed until 15 June following a settlement of the strike on the previous evening.

Following the departure of 2-8-2T No 5203, (the last locomotive to receive a repair) from the Works yard on Tuesday 16 April 1963 operations at Caerphilly had come to an end, the works formally closing after Friday 28 June 1963, its last day of operation. On that day, 0-6-0PT No 9480 was at the head of the last works train, which at that time had been reduced to three coaches, detonators being placed on the track from beyond the Goods Yard, to the junction of the main lines approaching Caerphilly station.

Below:
The practice at the Wolverhampton factory was to keep locomotives at Stafford Road (84A) MPD prior to entry. Here, former GWR 0-6-0PT No 7711 (L90) has arrived for inspection in March 1962. This was the first locomotive to carry the number L90. Later that year 0-6-0PT No 7760 received a Light Intermediate repair and took the place of No 7711 as L90 which was then withdrawn *M.A. Collins*

Bottom:
Collett-designed 0-6-0PT No 7444 is seen at Stafford Road MPD in September 1961. Entering the factory on 10 August 1961 No 7444 received a Heavy General repair and was outshopped in plain black livery, she was returned to Carmarthen (87G) MPD on 13 September.

The late K. Cooper/Colour-Rail

FOUR

WOLVERHAMPTON

Stafford Road Locomotive Works, often referred to as just Stafford Road, had its origins in the Shrewsbury & Birmingham Railway and by 1847 this company, already resigned to not reaching Birmingham by its own line, had decided to make its headquarters at Wolverhampton. This would offer some form of locomotive repair and accommodation facility. In particular they were looking for a site within easy access of their line. At that time Wolverhampton was built as far as Fox's Lane and a quarter of a mile further on, at Gosbrook, an auxiliary was being built and left a prime site ready for infilling. Duly purchased by the S & B, construction of the locomotive works did not commence until 1849. The first development was between the west side of Stafford Road and the S&B main line and was opened in November of that year.

Like the GWR at Swindon, the S&B were far from satisfied with the products of independent locomotive builders and appointed the Hon Edmund Petre as Inspector at their works. After rebuilding four of their 0-4-2 tender goods engines, he left in 1854 and was succeeded by Joseph Armstrong, who left his position as Locomotive Superintendent of the Shrewsbury & Chester Railway.

Following amalgamation of the S&B and S&C with the GWR from 1 September 1854, Daniel Gooch, the GWR's Locomotive Superintendent, decided to centralise locomotive repairs of their Northern Division at Stafford Road, at the same time submitting plans for additions and alterations to the then present shops. Before undertaking these improvements, he appointed Joseph Armstrong as Superintendent from which followed a lengthy period of conversion of the repair shops into a locomotive works. Armstrong also brought with him his brother George from the S&C and in October 1855 took on one William Dean as a pupil.

By 1859 the additions and alterations were far enough advanced for Joseph Armstrong to begin locomotive construction to his own design. In September 1859, the works completed its first completely new locomotives, the 2-2-2 express singles Nos 7 and 8. Little locomotive building at Stafford Road took place after that due to its mixed roles of locomotive maintenance and construction. Following amalgamation of the West Midland Railway with the GWR matters came to a head when the total narrow gauge locomotive stock had risen to 301. To add additional capacity to the existing work site there was some vacant space adjacent to the Broad Gauge running shed giving room for new erecting, fitting and machine shops, the Broad Gauge shed later becoming a tender shop.

Upon the retirement of Daniel Gooch as the GWR's Locomotive Superintendent in 1854, the Directors appointed Joseph Armstrong to the position and left his brother George in charge at Stafford Road with William Dean as his Assistant and Works Manager. Over the next 33 years Armstrong began a major programme of locomotive rebuilding whenever an engine became due for repair. This he operated alongside a programme of new locomotive construction using the same components. During this period he increased the number of locomotives built at Stafford Road by 600. Armstrong developed what became known as the Wolverhampton style with more than just livery differences. Different features included narrower chimneys with more rounded rolled copper tops as well as flat or dished smokebox doors. Even more noticeable were the Wolverhampton boilers, each with a tall brass dome and very apparent were the Armstrong cabs, or the lack of them - a flat weatherboard with two circular windows in it. The origins of the `Wolverhampton livery´ lay in the Oxford, Worcester & Wolverhampton Railway,

which had used a deep blue-green for painting locomotive and tender bodywork. With boiler bands and body panels lined in black edged with white, the wheels, frames and coupling rods were painted in a dark purple-brown. This livery remained virtually unaltered until 1902 when `Swindon´ livery became the norm.

Having completed the remainder of a large order for 160 0-6-0 saddle tanks in 1905, Stafford Road was called upon in that year to construct 10 of the Churchward 2-6-2 tank locomotives of the `3101´ class. As with all other new locomotives built at Stafford Road, these were constructed in the new two-road engine shop. The main problem following construction was getting the locomotives out of the shop. This necessitated removing their pony trucks and then by a gang of men with pinch bars through a hole knocked in the end of the wheel shop. Consequently, after completing an order for a further 20 of these machines, these problems dictated that no more orders for new locomotives would be placed at Stafford Road.

With government finance available for the relief of unemployment under their `Loans and Guarantees´ Act of 1929, the GWR put together a package totalling 200,000 man months, financing which made possible the reconstruction and modernisation of Stafford Road. The main new building to be constructed was an erecting shop, work progressing through 1930 and 1931. With this and many other modernisations, Stafford Road was transformed from a rundown Victorian establishment into a modern locomotive repair depot, all in little over three years.

The British Railways Modernisation Plan, published in 1955, gave evidence that steam locomotive repair facilities, such as those at Stafford Road, had only a short future, the Plan opting for diesel traction. It was obvious to many that further changes would be likely at the works, but few were prepared for the statement issued by the British Transport Commission on 26 May 1959 which announced that the whole works would close. This closure would have meant the loss of some 600 jobs and on hearing this Wolverhampton Town Council passed a resolution of alarm at its June 1959 meeting. Whether this was ever heard at the BTC will never be known, but on 15 July 1959, plans for resiting a diesel repair works at Stafford Road were announced. News in January 1960 brought further encouragement in that the diesel work could provide employment for up to 300 and that steam repair work would continue longer than expected. Later in the year, on 3 September, came the news that everyone wanted to hear - that Stafford Road works would not close - it would maintain and repair diesels. However, after continuing optimistically through 1961 and the first half of 1962, the announcement came from the BTC that there would be a general reduction of 20,000 in the workforce at its main railway workshops over the next five years - exact details being given later. After much lobbying by Local Trades Councils, the BTC agreed to reprieve some 3,000 jobs nationwide, but this did not save Stafford Road. Notice of final closure came on 21 August 1963 and decreed that the works would cease to function from 1 June 1964.

On 11 February 1964, GWR 2-8-0 No 2859 had the dubious distinction of being the last locomotive to be overhauled at Stafford Road. After setting-off back to its home depot at Pontypool Road (86G), No 2859 left the remaining 130 employees with nothing to do.

Right:
Bulleid `Battle of Britain´ 4-6-2 No 34082 *615 Squadron* is seen outside Eastleigh MPD in its rebuilt condition on 18 April 1964. Entering traffic in September 1948, No 34082 spent many years operating on the South Eastern division until reallocation to Nine Elms (70A) MPD in October 1961. In September 1964 *615 Squadron* was allocated to Eastleigh (70D) MPD, where she remained until withdrawn in September 1966. *W. Potter*

Below:
The fine appearance of Maunsell design `Lord Nelson´ 4-6-0 No 30856 *Lord St Vincent* is displayed in this view taken outside Eastleigh Works on 18 September 1960. Introduced in 1926 the sixteen members of the class had four cylinders (16^{1}/$_{2}$in diam x 26in long) the crank setting giving eight small blasts per revolution. *T.B. Owen*

Left:
Ivatt 2-6-2T No 41283 is seen outside Eastleigh shed following repair in March 1963. Owing to regional changes after 1957, many of these locos were allocated to sheds on all of the regions with the exception of the Scottish, No 41283 being reallocated from Patricroft (26F) MPD to Brighton (75A) MPD in June 1961. At the time this picture was taken, No 41283 was once again being reallocated, this time to Barnstaple Junction (72E) MPD. *Roy Hobbs*

FIVE

EASTLEIGH

At the turn of the century, the LSWR drawing office still occupied the site at Nine Elms. At that time the company had a virtual monopoly of the holiday traffic all along the south coast from Southsea and the Isle of Wight to Exmouth and had routes spread along the north coasts of both Devon and Cornwall, as well as to Plymouth. Beyond Exeter, its arch rival, the Great Western had a similar monopoly along the south coasts of both Devon and Cornwall. However, the `bucket and spade´ traffic was not the only commitment of the LSWR, for there were also the large military establishments at Aldershot and on Salisbury Plain. In addition to this there was naval traffic to both Portsmouth and Plymouth as well as the traffic to the fast growing port of Southampton, which was shortly to become Britain´s premier passenger port.

At this time the South Western´s motive power resources were somewhat limited, with much traffic still in the hands of the elderly Adams 4-4-0 classes of which the `T9´ class were excellent engines and performed admirably for many years. However, they were only of modest dimensions and their capacity to handle trains on the Exeter road was somewhat limited. The `T9s´ were eventually replaced by the larger `L12´ 4-4-0s which entered service in 1904. Even before these entered service Drummond had decided upon a large boilered 4-6-0 to meet the LSWR´s demand for more powerful locomotives. This was Class `F13´ No 330, a large-boilered 4-6-0 with four cylinders which was the first of five to appear in 1905. However, with hindsight, these turned out to be wretched engines which failed to meet the bill on the Salisbury to Exeter express passenger work, ending their days in unglamorous goods haulage.

By 1910, the LSWR had completed its new locomotive works at Eastleigh, the men and plant being transferred from Nine Elms. In September of that year the first locomotive was outshopped, Class `S14´ 0-4-0 Motor Tank No 101. One aim of the move had been to speed up the overhaul of the company´s locomotive stock and to reduce costs with more efficient workshop facilities, in what Dugald Drummond claimed to be `the most complete and up-to-date works owned by any railway company´. They were designed for the conduct of repairs and overhauls on a progressive basis - ie parts and materials were handled in such a way that they covered the shortest route and did not have to retrace their paths to get from one shop to another. All of these activities were moved as part of an overall programme.

Following the construction of the Class `S14´ Motor Tank, came the four-cylinder design `T14´ class, popularly known as the `Paddleboxes´. These were a great improvement over their predecessors but inherited too many of the basic Drummond defects in design. For all their shortcomings, they might have been very good engines had they been given boilers no larger than on his big 4-4-0, the `D15´ class. Built for the Bournemouth road which called for a high degree of boiler capacity and continuous steam output, unfortunately the `Paddleboxes´ did not fit the bill. As free running locomotives they ran well enough, but there was a definite limit to the load they could haul over the route.

In the last year of his life, Drummond gave the LSWR his masterpiece, his `D15´ 4-4-0s Nos 463-72. Here was a large enough boiler, matched with large cylinders, inside the frames, with piston valves and Walschaert gear and more importantly, outside admission valves. These engines were a match for the Bournemouth services with help in later years from the Urie `N15´ 4-6-0s.

Following the Drummond era, there followed a revolutionary era of design at Eastleigh with the appointment of Robert Wallace Urie, another dour Scot. He had been Drummond´s Works Manager for years and accordingly, having had to grapple with the four-cylinder monstrosities, he opted to design for strength and simplicity. These two elements were to form the basis for all his locomotive types. The main frames cut from 1¹/₄in plate, were the heaviest yet used on any British loco and in place of the inadequate steel axleboxes used by Drummond, he chose to use large manganese brass bearings with white metal lining. Whilst they were heavy and expensive, they lasted, and even after the normal spell of 75,000 miles between General repairs they often required only minimal attention.

From these concepts evolved his `H15´ 4-6-0s, the first, No 486, entering traffic in January 1914. It was the outbreak of World War 1 that stopped new locomotive construction at Eastleigh until 1918, when the expected express passenger version of the `H15´ appeared with 6ft 7in wheels and a taper boiler. Of a similar design were the 20 `S15s´, Nos 496-515 built between 1920-21. Other Urie contributions were the massive `G16´ 4-8-0Ts built for working the humps in a new marshalling yard being built at Feltham and the similar `H16´ 4-6-2Ts which were for operating the transfer goods trains between Feltham and other London sorting yards.

At the Grouping, Urie, being 68 years old, declined the position of Chief Mechanical Engineer to the Southern Railway, the choice of the SR directors falling upon Richard Edward Lloyd Maunsell, then CME of the South Eastern & Chatham Railway. He was quick to recognise that he had an excellent machine in the Urie `N15´ 4-6-0 using the latest practices, which included raising the boiler pressure to 200 lb/sq in. On top of that he introduced larger piston valves with a lengthening of the valve travel. The results were more than satisfactory to justify an order for a further 30 to be built by the North British Locomotive Co and a further 14 which were eventually built at Eastleigh.

Without doubt, Maunsell´s finest design was the `Schools´ class 4-4-0 which made much use of standard parts and a shortened version of the `King Arthur´ boiler. The motion was entirely `Lord Nelson´ and a three-cylinder arrangement was adopted, making this hybrid a highly successful machine. Maunsell´s final design was the `Q´ class 0-6-0, a locomotive designed to fill the gap between the ageing `Black Motors´ and the 4-6-0 goods. This class, introduced in 1938, finally numbered 20 examples.

Retiring in 1937, Richard Maunsell was succeeded by Oliver Bulleid as Chief Mechanical Engineer of the Southern Railway. One of his first actions was to introduce a new `Malachite´ colour scheme and also to make some improvements to his predecessor´s engines (in particular the 'Lord Nelsons') in order to improve their performance. Bulleid was nothing if not controversial during his term of office and one of his most startling actions during the darkest years of World War 2 was the introduction of a new concept in express passenger motive power. This new 4-6-2 had 6ft 2in driving wheels and could be just described as a mixed traffic locomotive in order to get round wartime sensitivity on these matters. It was little if not fully streamlined although described as air-smoothed for much the same reason. Possibly influenced by Bulleid´s term as Gresley´s assistant in the pre-1937 period, it was constructed with a three-cylinder arrangement.The new `Merchant Navy´ Pacific, was literally bristling with new ideas - not least being the unorthodox chain drive valve gear. Twenty examples were built by the Southern and a further 10 after Nationalisation. When running well these engines were magnificent but maintenance and other problems put them in a lesser light. It was not unexpected that the LMS dominated BR team chose to rebuild them on more conventional lines with three sets of orthodox valve gear. It is worth recording that most of the design work for the rebuilding was undertaken at Brighton whilst the casting of the inside cylinders was undertaken at Crewe, the machining being completed at Ashford.

With the closure of Ashford Works in 1962, all its repair work was transferred to Eastleigh and in the same year Eastleigh became part of BR workshops division. At that time there were some 1,500 employees at Eastleigh, a number which did not include those employed in the near-by Carriage and Wagon works. When the original works were built at Eastleigh, bays 1 to 4 were all erecting shop bays, totalling 67 engine repair pits, but more efficient repair methods resulted in locomotives returning to traffic in much shorter times. With engines running for much longer periods between overhauls and the typical turn round time for repairs to a `Merchant Navy´ being reduced to 22 days, other shops were

moved into the space that had been freed. A new diesel repair shop was added for the repair of engines used in SR multiple units, 350hp shunters and 204hp shunters.

In the wheel shop a wheel-welding machine, the first of its kind on BR was used for building up the outside diameters of old wheels. This operation was undertaken when, after successive retyrings, they had been machined to less than the minimum repair size for tyres, the process renewing their active life, while keeping them within the normal range of tyre bores. This shop also had ultrasonic equipment for detecting flaws in axles, systematic checking of locomotives´ axles and crank pins being undertaken as they proceeded through the shops.

The standard of workmanship from Eastleigh Locomotive Works has often been acknowledged to be of a high order and has continued well into the diesel electric era. This was undoubtedly due to a well equipped and keenly run apprentice training school which was introduced in 1958. Here, apprentices were given a grounding in a number of trades and today the works continues repairs for the entire Southern Region. In 1970 Eastleigh became part of British Rail Engineering Ltd and in April 1987 became a Level 5 depot as part of British Rail Maintenance Ltd.

Bulleid `Merchant Navy´ No 35004 *Cunard White Star* **is seen inside Eastleigh Works on 6 July 1958. At this time No 35004 had received a Heavy General repair and rebuilt to non-streamlined form. Officially returned to traffic on 5 July 1958, it could be suggested that the locomotive had been swiftly returned into Works after tests in the yard.**

T.B. Owen

Above:
Exmouth Junction's Unrebuilt `Battle of Britain´ Pacific No 34079 *141 Squadron* is depicted at Eastleigh MPD following repair on 9 May 1959. Built at Brighton in July 1948, No 34079 never carried the Bulleid numbering scheme and had amassed some 765,302 miles up until recording ceased in late 1964. The apparent quality of this particular picture is due to the fact that the photographer used a Polarising Filter to remove the large amount of unwanted reflected light that was catching the large streamlined side panels. *T.B. Owen*

Below:
Designed by Adams for the LSWR, BR Class `G6´ 0-6-0T No 30277 is depicted outside Eastleigh shed on 24 September 1955. The class was introduced in 1894, No 30277 being built in April 1900. They were mainly used for shunting in yards and when constructed they were fitted with heavier buffer beams, a shunter's footboard and handrail abreast the bunker side. Some members of the class were employed for banking up the 48 chains of 1 in 37 between Exeter St Davids and Exeter Central prior to being displaced by the class E1/R 0-6-2Ts. *T.B. Owen*

LSWR class T9 `Greyhound´ 4-4-0 No 120 is seen on the rollers inside Eastleigh works on 3 March 1962. Repainted to LSWR 1918 livery and still in operational service, No 120 operated on enthusiast specials until formally retired in July 1963. *T.B. Owen*

Below:
Arriving at Eastleigh for repair on 10 June 1963, Exmouth Junction´s Ivatt 2-6-2T No 41284 is depicted with all wheels removed inside the Works. Dispatched on 6 July 1963, No 41284 remained at Exmouth Junction until reallocated to Weymouth (70G) MPD in September 1964.
R. Hobbs

Bottom:
This superb interior view taken inside Eastleigh Works shows rebuilt `West Country´ 4-6-2 No 34034** *Honiton* **receiving its final coat of paint before return to traffic. Other locomotives in view are `West Country´ 34016 *Bodmin* **and Class Q 0-6-0 No 30544. Formerly numbered 21C134,** *Honiton* **was rebuilt in August 1960.** *J.P. Mullett/Colour-Rail*

Built for the LSWR at Eastleigh in February 1921, 'S15' 4-6-0 No 30512 has been specially prepared to haul an LCGB Railtour and was photographed approaching Alton on 3 November 1963. *T.B. Owen*

'Battle of Britain' No 34064 *Fighter Command* is depicted outside Eastleigh shed on 9 May 1964. No 34064 was fitted with a Giesl Ejector during a visit to Eastleigh in April 1962. During the same visit it was also coupled to modified tender T3314. *A.N.H. Glover*

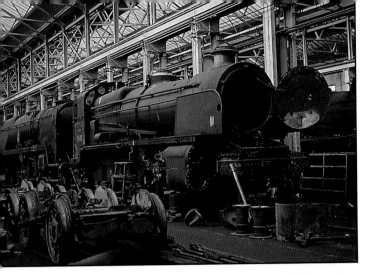

Left:
Built at Ashford in June 1920, `N´ class 2-6-0 No 31811 was one of a batch of 15 of this type constructed between 1920 and 1923. This batch was allocated to Bricklayers Arms, Tonbridge and Ashford MPDs and were more often used on goods traffic than passenger. Here, No 31811 is receiving attention inside the shops at Eastleigh in April 1963. Also present in this view is `West Country´ Pacific No 34056 Croydon. R. Hobbs

Left:
`King Arthur´ Class N15 4-6-0 No 30453 King Arthur is inside Eastleigh Works on 6 July 1959. One of the series 448-457 introduced in 1925, No 453 had increased boiler pressure, smaller firebox, long-travel valves and received a distinctive inside bearing tender from a withdrawn Drummond `G14´ 4-6-0. T.B. Owen

Below:
Unrebuilt `Merchant Navy ´ 4-6-2 No 35013 Blue Funnel is depicted outside Eastleigh shed on 27 March 1954. Built at Eastleigh as 21C13, No 35013 had completed 517,915 miles when rebuilt in May 1956. Surviving until July 1967, No 35013 had brought her total mileage in traffic up to 1,114,658 when withdrawn. T.B. Owen

Above:

Stanier `8F´ 2-8-0 No 48773 is seen outside Eastleigh Works on 25 August 1957. A locomotive with a remarkably chequered history, it was built as WD 307 and had seen considerable service in the Middle East before being sold to BR. After overhaul she was dispatched to Polmadie (66A) MPD and still needing works attention, was subsequently sent all the way to Eastleigh. Holding the distinction of being the last locomotive in steam at Rose Grove MPD on 4 August 1968, No 48773 survives today on the Severn Valley Railway. *R.C. Riley*

Left:

WD 2-10-0 No 601 *Kitchener* was photographed outside Eastleigh MPD on 15 September 1963. No 601 together with BR Standard Class 5 4-6-0 No 73049 remained on shed following an Open Day at the Works on the previous day.
Ray Reed

Left:

Transferred to Southern Region stock when reallocated from Cardiff Cathays (88A) MPD to Nine Elms (70A) MPD on 14 June 1959, Ex-WR 0-6-0PT No 4698 is depicted outside Eastleigh shed. After that date all service and maintenance was the responsibility of the Southern Region. *D. Penney*

41

Above:

Carrying the small BR `Lion & Wheel´ logo, `King Arthur´ Class N15 No 30750 *Morgan le Fay* stands outside Eastleigh shed on 24 September 1955. Built by the LSWR at Eastleigh in October 1922, this class were the first LSWR locomotives to be constructed with a taper boiler. Contrary to the practice largely established by the GWR, only the front boiler ring was tapered, and the second, or rearward, ring was made parallel.

T.B.Owen

Left:

SR Class Z 0-8-0T No 30950 is seen under repair inside Eastleigh Works on 18 September 1960. Ordered from Brighton Works in March 1926, the eight 0-8-0Ts did not appear until March-September 1929, an order for a further 10 being cancelled in view of the depressed economic situation. When new, they were tested up the steep 1 in 30 grade of the Folkestone Harbour branch. However, with the cancellation of the order for the further 10, there were no `Zs´ available for this duty. Best known for their work on banking duties at Exeter, no example of the class survives, although one, No 30952, was noted in store at Fratton shed along with other locomotives that would form part of the National Collection.

T.B. Owen

Left:

Former `B4´ class 0-4-0T No 30102 is depicted outside Eastleigh Works on 29 September 1964. Cosmetically restored for display at Billy Butlin´s Skegness holiday camp, this locomotive can now be seen on exhibition at Bressingham Steam Museum. One of 25 members of the class designed by Adams and built for the LSWR at Nine Elms Works, the first example appeared in 1891. Originally numbered 406 it later carried Southern Railway Nos E102 and 102 and was named *Granville*. Mainly used for dock shunting, it was one of two members of the class to be preserved. The other example, No 30096, was purchased by the Bulleid Preservation Society and can be seen in traffic on the Bluebell Railway.

J. Duncan Gomersall

Above:
Class O2 0-4-4T No 30200 is seen inside Eastleigh shed on 30 March 1957. Designed by Adams for the LSWR and built at Nine Elms Works between 1889 and 1895, the class was introduced to replace the Beattie well-tanks on branch line and short distance passenger work. No 30200 worked from Wadebridge from 1957 until March 1961 when it was re-allocated to Eastleigh becoming one of the last four members of the class to survive on the mainland. Another 19 members of the class remained operational on the Isle of Wight and continued to haul their rakes of antiquated coaches until December 1966. *T.B. Owen*

Below:
Taken out of service for a General repair on 23 May 1962, Bulleid `Merchant Navy´ 4-6-2 No 35022 *Holland-America Line* is depicted outside the Works on 4 August 1962. With repairs having been completed by 28 July, it is probable that the locomotive had not returned to Exmouth Junction (72A) MPD until after Eastleigh Works Open Day which was held on 1 August. Carrying the Brunswick Green livery since December 1952, No 35022 completed some 329,083 miles in traffic before being rebuilt in June 1956 and achieved a total of 903,542 miles before being withdrawn in May 1966. *G.W. Morrison*

Marsh Class `H2` Atlantic No 32424 *Beachy Head* is seen outside Brighton shed on 13 April 1958 after hauling the `Sussex Coast Limited` railtour from Victoria to Newhaven harbour. No 32424 had made a brief visit to Eastleigh Works in August 1956 and spent much of its time on the through Bournemouth service before being laid aside at Brighton on 24 February 1957. Withdrawal would have probably occurred at the end of that month had it not been requested to work the `Sussex Coast Limited` railtour.
T.B. Owen

SIX

BRIGHTON

Joining the London, Brighton & South Coast Railway as Locomotive Superintendent in 1847, John Chester Craven created Brighton Works as a centre of locomotive building. Having gained experience in the moving of the Eastern Counties Railway's works from Romford to Stratford, it was his responsibility to expand their somewhat cramped site on the east side of the main line immediately north of the passenger station. By 1852 the works produced its first home-built locomotives - two small single driver well tanks. The first of a great variety of locomotives built under the Craven regime, the classes were small in numbers and needed their own spare parts. By the time William Stroudley took over from Craven in 1870, the LBSCR was said to have had 72 different classes in use, a number which included locomotives bought from outside in the early years, and which had been adapted and modified to suit Craven´s requirements. On taking the reins as Locomotive Superintendent, Stroudley set about cutting down the number of spare parts that had become necessary to keep such a wide variety of locomotives in traffic. His policy was to introduce six standard classes which would have a large number of interchangeable parts, so that a relatively small stock of spares would be required, thus minimising the time locomotives spent under repair in Works. As soon as he had taken office, Stroudley began large scale reorganisation. He had carriage and wagon building transferred from the west side of the line to the main works site on the east and moved the locomotive depot to to the west, thus taking advantage of the additional space made by the removal of a chalk hill. The previous erecting shop constructed by Craven was turned into a smithy, a new one being constructed.

Upon his death in 1889, Stroudley was succeeded by R.J. Billinton. Under his aegis the LBSCR locomotive stock expanded rapidly from 410 in 1890 to 535 by 1902. Billinton continued Stroudley´s policies of standardisation and also began the practice of storing spare boilers. The problems of space at the works continued obliging Billinton to build new accommodation over the goods lines on the eastern side, supporting the new floor space on brick piles. Even so, congestion remained a problem, Billinton´s 0-6-0 goods engines being sub-contracted to the Vulcan Foundry. The class later acquired the name `Vulcans´. In 1892 the erecting shop was almost doubled in length, two tracks extending from end to end. During Billinton´s day the option of moving the carriage and wagon work away from Brighton was considered and it was eventually moved to a site at Lancing, between Shoreham and Worthing, the new depot becoming operational in 1912.

In 1905 D. Earle Marsh took over from Billinton. He continued the process of internal reorganisation, and when the works at Lancing were completed, the wagon shop was handed over to the Locomotive Department for running repairs. The last Locomotive Superintendent of the LBSCR was L.B. Billinton (son of R.J.) who took office in 1911. With demands for larger motive power, the works moved into the `Big Engine´ era, the main block being extended to 600ft long and 450ft wide at its largest point, narrowing towards the boundary with New England Road.

During World War 1, the works contributed to the war effort with munitions production and other work, the end of the war leaving a somewhat uncertain outlook. By 1923, the LBSCR had become the Central Section of the Southern Railway, the last locomotive to be constructed under the LBSCR being the 4-6-4T No 333 *Remembrance*.

In the early years of the Grouping Brighton Works came under the direction of R.E.L. Maunsell, the Southern Railway´s first Chief Mechanical Engineer. In 1926 10 of the `River´ class 2-6-4Ts were constructed at Brighton, these being followed in 1928 by 10 `U´ class 2-6-0s, and in 1929 came the eight powerful `Z´ class 0-8-0Ts. After this period much of the work done at Brighton was transferred to Ashford and Eastleigh although the works continued to carry out running repairs to locomotives, coaches, and eventually EMU stock. However, production was to return to Brighton in 1942 when activity on war work meant that the works was totally re-equipped, locomotive construction resuming with 2-8-0 freight locomotives which it supplied to the War Office at the incredible rate of one every 4.5 days. Military work included component parts for tanks and anti-aircraft defence .Towards the end of hostilities, locomotive construction continued in the form of 104 Bulleid Light Pacifics. The 1,000th new locomotive to be built at Brighton being Bulleid Pacific No 34064 *Fighter Command*.

Having tested his sleeve valve gear on converted Atlantic No 32039 *Hartland Point,* O.V.S. Bulleid´s `Leader´ class locomotive No 36001 was built at Brighton under a curtain of absolute secrecy. The first and only member of its class, it finally went to the scrap heap. However Brighton did eventually move into the diesel age by building the Southern Regions´s 1Co-Co1 diesel-electric No 10203, which emerged from the works in 1953.

By 1952, its centenary year, Brighton Works employed a staff of about 650 and covered nine acres. The boiler shop was then in two bays each served by cranes of 30 tons and 20 tons capacity. At the south end both bays were spanned by a 30-ton electric crane which was used for lifting boilers for riveting in a 90-ton riveting machine which was powered by a self-contained hydraulic system. Portable milling and grinding machines were operated by compressed air and high-speed machines for the drilling and tapping of fireboxes were powered by a high-frequency (400Hz) electrical supply. Other equipment in the shop comprised a battery of radial drilling machines, plate levelling rollers and a plate edge planer for the preparation of plates before welding. Another large piece of equipment was the 250-ton flanging press served by a creosote/pitch fired furnace. At this time the erecting shop was also in two bays, locomotive repairs being concentrated in the west bay, served by travelling cranes of 40 tons, 35 tons and 25 tons capacity.

Visitors to Brighton at this time were often surprised to see a `Brighton yellow´ engine outside the works. This was the `Terrier ´ No 32635 in its Stroudley livery operating as 377S and lettered *Brighton Works.*

In post-Nationalisation years, the works designed and constructed some of the BR Standard steam locomotives including `9F´ 2-10-0s and 130 of the Standard Class `4´ 2-6-4Ts which included No 80154, outshopped on 20 March 1957, being the last steam locomotive to be turned out. After that date the rundown at Brighton Works began. Locomotive repair work continued until 1958, the work finally being transferred to Ashford and Eastleigh. After this date, some of the equipment and premises were used for motor car assembly. However, this was to be a short term reprieve, final closure coming in 1964 and demolition to clear the site for a car park beginning in 1969.

Above:
Brighton Works shunter, No DS 377, is depicted in its dark mustard yellow livery on 13 April 1958. Two years earlier it had received a coat of what could be described as Stroudley yellow ochre. Originally No 35 *Morden* in LBSCR days, it was returned to running stock in 1959 as 32635, and remaining at Brighton, it retained its special livery until it was withdrawn in March 1963. *T.B. Owen*

Below:
Class E4 0-6-2T No 32508 is seen outside Brighton shed on 13 April 1958. Designed by Robert Billinton for the LBSCR, the class was intended for use on short distance goods services, the first 12 being completed at a cost of £26,640 between December 1897 and August 1898. No 32508, originally numbered 508, was built in 1900 for a cost of £2,530.

T.B. Owen

Left:

Class R1 0-6-0T No 31337 is seen outside Ashford shed following repair at the Works in April 1958. Built for the South Eastern Railway (amalgamated in 1899 with the London, Chatham & Dover Railway to form the South Eastern & Chatham Railway) in 1888, three of the class were specifically intended for operation on the steeply graded Folkestone Harbour branch. No 31337 became one of the last five members of the class in operation, all being transferred to Nine Elms (70A) MPD in May 1959. *D. Penney*

Left:

Wainwright `D´ class 4-4-0 No 31744 has arrived at Ashford Works for breaking up. Introduced in May 1903, Nos 741 to 745 were built by the SECR by Robert Stephenson & Co (Works Nos 3083 to 3087). As the LMS designed 2-6-4Ts were being outshopped from Brighton Works in 1950-1951, there became progressively less work for the surviving members of the class. Today, Class D No 737 (BR No 31737) survives as part of the National Collection and is on display at the National Railway Museum at York. *T.B. Owen*

Below:

Wainwright SECR Class H 0-4-4T No 31193 is seen at the head of an RCTS railtour at East London Up Junction on 3 October 1959. Built at Ashford in 1909 as locomotive No 193, it was constructed as part of Wainwright's passenger tank programme (1904-1915) which was intended to replace the hitherto standard `Q´ class passenger tank and to cope with the continually increasing suburban traffic. *C.J. Gammell*

SEVEN

ASHFORD

It was in February 1846 that the Board of Directors of the South Eastern Railway decided to buy, for the sum of £21,000, from a gentleman of the name of Walls, 185 acres of good Kentish countryside, at Ashford, on which was to be sited - a `Locomotive Establishment´.

Having gained Parliamentary endorsement for a proposal to spend up to £500,000 on this new venture, the Directors reported to the proprietors that they had purchased the land on advantageous terms, and in the situation they wished to have. By the summer of 1847 a cluster of 72 labourers´ cottages had been built on the site and the story of Ashford Works had begun. An imaginative conception, the `Railway Village´, as it was later to become, possessed its own general shop, its own public baths, its airy, spacious green on the doorsteps of the workpeople´s homes and even its own `Pub´, not nearly so Gradgrind-like as some of today´s employers.

From the beginning of 1847, a limited amount of repair and maintenance work had been undertaken and it was to be the following year, 1848, that was to see construction begin on the first locomotive. This remarkable little engine, completed in 1850, had a vertical boiler and was nicknamed the `Coffee Pot´. Its design was attributed to a marine engineer called Fernihough. Used for propelling the Company Directors and Chief Engineers about the South Eastern system and it was active in railway service until 1861 when it was taken off the line to do pump house service at Redhill. By 1851 the Works was supporting some 3,000 people, including employees´ wives and children.

For several years the destiny of the locomotive department of the South Eastern Railway was in the capable hands of James I´Anson Cudworth. His first 2-4-0 passenger engines had outside frames and a compensating beam above the bearings, and gained a creditable reputation under the title of the `Hastings´ or `157´ class. An experimenting engineer, it was he who introduced the `Uniflow´ system of steam distribution to a railway engine. In addition to this he developed a firebox divided by a longitudinal water partition, or `Midfeather´, a device with sloping grates which made it possible for coal fuel to be used without the emission of smoke. Hitherto, the staple diet of a railway engine´s firebox had been coke. Eventually all engines in Cudworth´s charge were fitted with this firebox, a device that remained standard on the South Eastern´s locomotives for the next 30 years - that is until 15 years after Cudworth had retired. After building a number of various goods and passenger engines, Cudworth introduced his `Mail´ class locomotives. These 7ft `Singles´ were introduced to haul the fast London-Dover `Post Office´ expresses. It was to be the commissioning of Ramsbottom, of the LNWR, to design a passenger engine that caused Cudworth to resign, his position being taken by the son of the Chairman, Mr A.M. Watkin. His only contribution to the South Eastern´s motive power was his name which was commonly bestowed on the 20 Ramsbottom locomotives. Watkin´s successor was R.C. Mansell, who had been Carriage and Wagon Superintendent during this time. He had already brought distinction to the South Eastern with his `Mansell ´ wheel for carriage stock. This successful Ashford innovation was composed of a steel tyre with teak segments which was forced on to the axles by a 60-ton hydraulic press. Three other locomotive classes were introduced under Mansell during his interim term of office until the arrival of James Stirling, straight from the north, firm disciplinarian and railway pioneer. He was a designer who saw no need for the steam dome and consequently all loco-

motives that came out of Ashford at this time were without this traditional feature. He was greatly esteemed amongst the staff at the Works and his first passenger locomotives were 4-4-0s with 6ft driving wheels. After building various standard goods engines and a class of 0-4-4Ts, Ashford produced the initial model of his `F´ class bogie express engines with 7ft driving wheels. It was his inflexible aversion to photographers and their productions that few pictures exist of Stirling and the fine engines he created.

After Stirling came the Wainwright era at Ashford with a figure who had for the previous three years been in charge of the carriage and wagon section. During his years as Locomotive, Carriage and Wagon Superintendent, he produced some well-proportioned and resplendent engines. Highly polished brass dome coverings distinguished his creations, some classes being further embellished with copper-sheathed chimney tops. In an era of great productivity, the works at Longhedge and Battersea passed over their locomotive construction, and later their repair work, to Ashford. By 1909 there were 497 engines on the South Eastern section for which the works at Ashford were responsible.

Wainwright´s successor was R.E.L. Maunsell, the first to receive the title of `Chief Mechanical Engineer´. Although much of his early administration was connected with the manufacture of munitions, his first types of locomotive appeared in 1917 and were big departures from any of the types hitherto seen at Ashford. One class was a mixed-traffic 2-6-0 tender engine and the other, a 2-6-4 express passenger tank, both having outside cylinders. With the amalgamation of the railways in 1923, the last carriage built at Ashford rolled out of the shops, all carriage work being carried out at the erstwhile `Brighton´ company´s works at Lancing and the Eastleigh works of the other constituent company, the London & South Western. However, Ashford continued to build some very fine engines. In 1923 three of Maunsell´s highly successful 2-6-0s were turned out and in 1929, eight of his `U´ class engines steamed their way into service. An event in 1926 saw the visit of the future King and Queen, then of course, the Duke and Duchess of York. After a tour of the workshops it was the Duke who was at the regulator of Maunsell´s Eastleigh built `Lord Nelson´ - at that time the most powerful 4-6-0 in Britain - and drove the locomotive to Ashford station.

As a result of the opening of a new depot between the Canterbury and Folkestone lines in 1933, the Running shed was demolished. In the same year locomotive building boomed once again. Fifteen Maunsell `N´ Class 2-6-0s came out of the shops and seven large `W´ Class tank engines were built in 1935.

In 1937 Maunsell´s retirement saw the appointment of O.V.S. Bulleid as Chief Mechanical Engineer to the Southern Railway. World War 2 brought its share of problems to Ashford, as it brought its quota of bombs, with the German-occupied airfields in France a mere seven minutes´ flying time away. Notwithstanding the 2,881 `Red Warnings´ or the 2,044 spotters´ `Danger Signals´, war supplies poured out of the workshops. The surprising outlines of Mr Bulleid´s `Austerity´ 0-6-0s even became familiar in the Erecting shops and 14 of the powerful LMS-designed `8Fs´ were constructed in 12 months. By 1952 the works had built its last locomotive - an 0-6-0 diesel shunter and two years later, in 1954 , they undertook a major rebuilding of SR 2-6-0s with new cylinders and front ends. When Ashford became part of BR Workshops division in 1962, all locomotive work was transferred to Eastleigh.

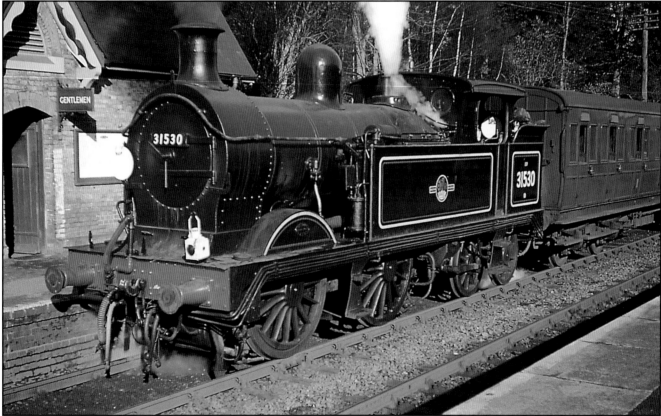

Brighton (75A) MPD´s `Schools´ class 4-4-0 No 30901 *Winchester*
appears in splendid condition outside Ashford Works as sister class
member No 30910 *Merchants´s Taylors* **awaits attention on 20 June 1960.**
For this class, the largest 4-4-0s in Europe, Maunsell had made use of
standard parts - the boiler was a shortened version of that used for the
`King Arthur´ and the motion was entirely `Nelson´. *R.C.Riley*

Above:
Ex-SECR `H´ class 0-4-4T prepares to depart from Rowfant with a
Three Bridges to East Grinstead auto train on 21 February 1960. Ex-
LSWR `M7´ 0-4-4Ts were periodically interchanged with the `Hs´ on
this service, but were not popular with the Three Bridges crews. Latterly
BR Standard Class 4 2-6-4Ts were to replace the pre-Grouping 0-4-4Ts,
steam being eventually ousted by DEMUs. *C.J. Gammell*

Top:
Constructed at Ashford in 1909, Tonbridge (74D) MPD´s `H´ class 0-4-4T No 31164 is depicted in Ex-Works condition outside Ashford (74A) MPD on 12 September 1954. Nos 264 and 312 were the first members of the class to be taken out of service in 1944, Nos 1184,1259,1530 and 1544 serving as air-raid shelters. *T.B. Owen*

Above:
`N´ class 2-6-0 No 31866 is being moved into position outside Ashford MPD on 6 March 1961. Ordered in 1923, No A866 (the last of the batch A846-75 to enter traffic) was specially prepared for display at the Wembley Exhibition, an event which postponed its debut on SR metals until 28 November 1925. *C.J. Gammell*

Above: **This general view taken on 13 May 1960 outside Ryde Works clearly shows the hoist which was often used for bogie changes. The mark left by a smokebox numberplate indicates that the replacement boiler originated from a mainland member of the `O2´ class.**
J.P. Mullett/Colour-Rail

Below: **The only member of the `O2´ class to survive into preservation, No 24 *Calbourne* was photographed at Easter 1958 outside Ryde MPD. With the exception of heavy boiler repairs, the works at Ryde were virtually self-sufficient, and carried out complete overhauls to both locomotives and rolling stock alike.** *D. Penney*

EIGHT

RYDE (I.O.W.)

One of the smallest, yet one of the most interesting locomotive workshops in the country, its lack of size was certainly compensated for by the quality of its work. It is something of a miracle that the aged engines and carriages managed to carry the heavy summer loads and the entire credit must go to the craftsmen at the works. The last steam locomotive to be overhauled at the works was No 27 *Merstone* at the end of July 1966 and the last steam-hauled coach was No 2442 which left the carriage shops in mid July.

The original works were built by the Isle of Wight Railway Co, the oldest part being the locomotive erecting shop on which work was believed to have commenced in 1864. As at Swindon, the stone used was obtained from tunnelling activities, the stone for Ryde coming from excavations in the construction of Ventnor tunnel. A second brick built locomotive shop was later added. On the roof of the older shop, a water tank inscribed IWR 1870 was supplied by means of a windmill which pumped from Monkton Mead brook. This water was also used to feed locomotives on the down platform and in the engine shed. Obviously this method of supplying water ceased with the introduction of town water. There was also a boiler house with a brick chimney which was demolished in 1924. The old carriage and wagon repair shop was a wooden structure situated between the station and the locomotive shops. The layout in 1966 consisted of the two original locomotive shops and a new three-road carriage and wagon shop.

Both locomotive shops had a single road, the older erecting shop containing heavier equipment including two hammers and a machine for metal cutting. Most of the machinery was situated in the new shop and consisted of lathes, planing machines and radial drills. The largest machine was the wheel lathe used to reprofile tyres. Impressive to watch, it machined locomotive driving wheels but equally impressive to see in action was the 25 ton hoist which could raise a locomotive. The speed with which a pair of wheels or bogie could be changed was well worth seeing.

Engines repaired at Ryde over its 102 years maintaining steam were mainly the Beyer Peacock 2-4-0Ts in the early years of the owning company. Shortly after the Grouping, the Southern Railway concentrated all rolling stock repairs at Ryde and the Isle of Wight Central Railway's Works at Newport were closed for this purpose although they remained open as paint shops until 1959. Whilst this meant that the works at Ryde had to maintain a variety of locomotive types it was not until much later that these were reduced to three standard classes, the `O2´, `E1´ and `A1X´.

It was true to say that the equipment available in Ryde works did not match that to be found in some major mainland motive power depots and that these depots would not have been asked to carry out such major operations as lifting a locomotive boiler out of its frames. This operation had been carried out at Ryde for many years. The last locomotive to receive what could be described as a General repair was No 24 *Calbourne* which was made ready to operate in time for the summer 1965 timetable. It was plain for all to see that the quality of work carried out was of the highest standard bearing in mind the age of the locomotives and the limited facilities available. It can be said that out of three locomotives sent to the island after World War 2, none was still running by 1966, yet No 20 *Shanklin* was still at work after 40 years of Ryde maintenance. By 1966 only 11 engines were available to cover the eight passenger diagrams from Monday to Friday, with eight on Saturdays and four on Sundays. In official circles it was reported that the condition of locomotives then was better than that three years earlier before the ultrasonic testing of components had begun.

One important alteration to locomotive design appeared from Ryde Works in 1932. This was to a design by A.B. MacLeod which increased the capacity of the coal bunker to three tons, which was sufficient to allow a full day's running of nearly two hundred miles. The first locomotive to receive this modification was No 26 *Whitwell*, all others being dealt with as they became due for `shopping´. Other engines sent to the island were so equipped at Eastleigh Works before shipping.

Many famous engines passed through Ryde Works over the years. The first was the Beyer Peacock 2-4-0 T *Ryde* which was built for the opening of the Isle of Wight Railway in 1864. When withdrawn in 1932, it was the oldest working passenger locomotive on the Southern Railway and was removed to Eastleigh for preservation, but was broken up in the wartime drive for scrap metal. Another engine that was justly famous was No 11, a Stroudley `Terrier´. Formerly LBSCR No 40, *Brighton* had appeared at the 1878 Paris Exhibition. The Freshwater, Yarmouth & Newport Railway had only two engines: No 1 *Medina*, a Manning-Wardle saddle tank had the distinction of being the most modern Island locomotive taken over by the Southern in 1923, and for that matter since. This engine had been used for shunting at Medina Wharf and for general goods and mineral work; the FYNR No 2 also had a chequered history. It had operated on no fewer than five different railways before ending its days on the Hayling Island branch. Together with IWCR No 10, this engine was rebuilt at Ryde Works from Class A1 to Class A1X. One machine built at Ryde Works in 1932 to a design by A.B. MacLeod was *Midget*, a geared manual tractor which sufficed to haul single loaded wagons in the yard and was in use until 1938. This machine was built entirely of scrap material.

A new carriage and wagon shop was erected in 1938. A spacious and well lit shop, it had 16ft of headroom and two roads, one 57ft long and the other 46ft. Because of the small number of coaches dealt with, Ryde Works often received cut-off rolls of carriage seating material from mainland workshops and as a result stocked a variety of patterns, some of which dated back to the days before Nationalisation. The carriages which lasted up until 1966 were all of pre-Southern Railway design, travelled smoothly and were very well upholstered, particularly those from the South Eastern & Chatham Railway. In an effort to increase the comfort in the third-class compartments of former LBSCR stock, a loose and wider rubber lined cushion was provided - a feature particular to the island.

A working life of 68 years for the locomotive *Ryde* was at one time a record, but by 1966, not one of the Isle of Wight engines was less than 74 years old. Of those the honour of being the oldest went to No 14 *Fishbourne*. The solid brass nameplates were removed in 1966, yet to replace these, the works provided cheaper, yet very distinctive replacements. This gesture gave much pleasure, not only to the local enthusiasts, but to all those who journeyed to see the last days of steam on the Isle of Wight.

Fortunately, one member of the `O2´ class, No 24 *Calbourne* survives in preservation on the Isle of Wight Steam Railway. Restored to working order it is currently undergoing repair.

Above:
Following an Intermediate repair, `Rebuilt Patriot´ No 45545 *Planet* is outside the Paint Shop at Crewe Works on 15 March 1959. During this repair No 45545 had been fitted with ATC equipment. *T.B. Owen*

Below:
Newly constructed `9F´ 2-10-0 No 92163 is depicted in primer alongside Stanier `Princess Royal´ Pacific No 46206 *Princess Marie Louise* on 23 February 1958. According to official records, No 92163 was formally in traffic at Kettering (15B) MPD the following day. *W. Potter*

NINE

CREWE

Celebrating its 150th anniversary only one year ago, Crewe Works were established by the Grand Junction Railway in 1843. Replacing the original works of the GJR at Edge Hill, they were built at Crewe in the `V´ formed by the lines to Chester and Warrington. Manufacturing locomotives, carriages and wagons, it had expanded from 30 to 50 acres during their first two years of operation.

Having taken over the Liverpool and Manchester Railway in 1845, the GJR merged with the London & Birmingham and Manchester & Birmingham railways in July 1846 thus forming the London & North Western Railway. This created what was to become the largest joint stock company in Britain, Crewe Works expanding to become the largest locomotive works in Britain which were wholly owned by an operating company. The new LNWR company operated in three divisions, roughly on the lines of the former constituents, each division retaining its former locomotive and carriage works, the Northern Division being served by Crewe. Within one year Crewe managed to delegate its responsibility for wagons to Edge Hill and just as history was to replay itself three quarters of a century later when the LNWR grouped with the L&Y and Midland to form the LMS, Directors of the constituent companies retained their partisan loyalties.

Having delegated all of its wagon production by 1853, Crewe also gave up its coach construction and repair facilities by 1859 when all Northern Division work was transferred to Saltley. At this time all locomotive construction at Wolverton ceased, the works concentrating solely on carriages with locomotive repairs ceasing over the successive 15 years. This left Crewe as the LNWR´s only locomotive works, the fleet growing from 949 locomotives to 3,100 by 1903. Unlike some other companies who had to sub-contract locomotive building and repair work, Crewe was totally self-sufficient, building every one of its own locomotives from the amalgamation of the Northern and Southern divisions right through until 1916 in the difficult times of World War 1.

The very first locomotive built at Crewe in 1843 for the GJR was an outside-cylinder type with double frames and inclined cylinders which became known as the `Crewe Type´. A total of 422 were built between 1843 and 1858, in 2-2-2 form for passenger work and as a 2-4-0 configuration for freight, the latter becoming known as the `Crewe Goods´.

Upon the retirement of Frances Trevithick in 1857, John Ramsbottom was appointed as his successor, the following year seeing the introduction of his `DX´ class of 0-6-0 express goods locomotives. By 1874, a grand total of 943 of these machines had been constructed, a total which was a record for any single class in Britain and included 86 for the Lancashire & Yorkshire Railway and two for the Portpatrick & Wigtownshire Railway. The Ramsbottom era at Crewe saw the introduction of standardised components, his `Lady of the Lake´ class sharing boiler-firebox assemblies, smokebox door and valve gear parts with his 2-2-2 `Problem´ and `DX´ classes. The new express 2-4-0 `Newton´ and `Samson´ class locomotives also shared many components with the `DX´ 0-6-0s. Throughout Ramsbottom´s period in office, the workshops at Crewe saw massive expansion and diversification and by 1870 were twice the size they had been a decade earlier. This growth had necessitated the construction of an 18in gauge internal tramway system, work having begun in 1861. At its greatest extent its track covered some five miles in length and by 1876 was operated by no fewer than seven narrow gauge locomotives. Upon retirement in 1871, Ramsbottom was succeed-

ed as Locomotive Superintendent by Francis William Webb whose reign saw brave innovations with experiments in compounding. By 1900 500 of his `Coal Class´ 0-6-0s had been constructed. Introduced in 1873 the `Coal Class´ were followed by the introduction of the `Cauliflower´ class in 1880, the 0-6-2T version of this class appearing in 1881. During the 1870s emerged the 2-4-0T `Choppers´ and a 2-4-2T of which many were rebuilds of the `Chopper´. But it was the passenger locomotives built at Crewe during the Webb era that were the most famous. The most outstanding of these were the 2-4-0 `Jumbo´ or `Precedent´ class that appeared between 1874 and 1882. It was in the latter year that the first of his experiments in compounding appeared in the form of the 2-2-2-0 `Experiment´ class and later the `Dreadnought´ class of the same configuration. Later in 1889 he constructed the 2-2-2-0 `Teutonics´ which had 7ft dia driving wheels. These locomotives were the most successful of his compound designs although there were problems with two later types having the 2-2-2-2-0 wheel arrangement. Also erratic in performance were his `Iron Duke ´ and `Alfred the Great´ 4-4-0s, but much more successful were his compound 0-8-0 freight locomotives. At that time these were the most successful freight locomotives in Britain, and were able to haul 940 tons south of Crewe.

Webb retired in 1903 and was succeeded by Whale who as CME disbanded the idea of compounding and his first passenger design appeared in 1904 in the form of the `Precursor´ class 4-4-0 of which 130 had been built by 1907. A fast 4-4-2T of this class appeared in 1906 for use on suburban passenger workings, this being the only `Atlantic´ to be built at Crewe. Whale´s reign at Crewe lasted only six years as he retired in 1909.

He was succeeded by C.J. Bowen Cooke, whose first passenger design was the `George the Fifth´ class 4-4-0, this being the first product from Crewe to use superheaters. A total of 90 of these were constructed between 1910 and 1915 and these were followed in 1911 by the `Prince of Wales´ class 4-6-0, a development of the `Experiment´´ class. The L&NWR´s final express passenger design was the four-cylinder simple expansion 4-6-0, the `Claughton´ class which were to give some sterling performances on the heavy West Coast main line expresses.

World War 1 brought a massive amount of munitions work to Crewe in addition to the maintenance and renewal of the locomotive fleet. The war was followed by a period of industrial unrest with a large backlog of repairs building up, some of which were given to outside contractors. When Bowen Cooke died in 1920 he was succeeded by Capt H. Beames who held the reins until the LNWR merged with the L&Y in 1922, when he was replaced by George Hughes from Horwich, a works well in advance of Crewe in terms of working practices and engine repair times. If his appointment had dented the pride of the `Premier Line´, this was to be nothing compared to the problems which arrived with the Grouping which saw the higher management of the LMS led by Midland Railway men, with their headquarters at Derby, who had been arch rivals of the L&NWR. Apart from an 0-8-4T version of the 0-8-2T Bowen Cooke tank, the next order at Crewe was for 150 examples of the Midland design `4F´ 0-6-0s being built by 1928, a further 15 being constructed by 1937.

With Hughes retiring in 1925, he was replaced by Sir Henry Fowler, former CME of the Midland Railway. The first standard LMS design was the 2-6-0 `Crab´ type, heavily based on L&Y practices, a total of

135 being built at Crewe between 1926 and 1935.

With the layout of the Works at Crewe being far from ideal, a major reorganisation was begun in 1925. A new erecting shop was constructed and the former L&Y steelworks at Horwich were closed with improved facilities taking their place at Crewe. However, with the economic climate of the depression, this did not last long and they were closed in 1932. All of the improvements led to locomotives taking 12 days instead of 32 to pass through for heavy repairs.

The early years of the LMS saw something of a crisis in top-link motive power and after trials in 1926 with the GWR 4-6-0 *Launceston Castle*, the rapid construction of the `Royal Scot´ class began. The first 50 of which were built by the North British Locomotive Company, the remaining 20 being built at Derby. This was followed in 1928 by the rebuilding of 20 `Claughtons´ with larger boilers. In 1931 Sir Henry Fowler moved sideways to become assistant to the vice president of the LMS and was briefly succeeded by E.J.H. Lemon who held the position until the appointment of William Stanier who was headhunted from the GWR.

At that time the LMS owned no locomotives capable of working a 500-ton express single handed throughout the 401 mile journey from London Euston to Glasgow. Taking up his appointment on 1 January 1932, Stanier´s remit was to produce a design to meet that requirement. Three prototype Pacifics were included in the construction programme, although the third was held back and was eventually completed as the turbine driven No 6202 Turbomotive. No 6200 *The Princess Royal* was completed by 27 June 1933 and, of course, William Stanier must take the credit. Between 1933 and 1937 he was responsible for producing the entire range of standard locomotives that came to serve the LMS so well:

`Princesses´, `Coronations´, `Jubilees´, `Black Fives´, `8F´ 2-8-0s and the various classes of passenger tanks. At the highest point of activity between 1935 and 1937 Crewe was replacing about 220 locomotives each year in an era which came to an end with the outbreak of World War 2. Just as in World War 1, Crewe undertook a significant level of war work, four Covenanter cruiser tanks being produced each week in addition to the repair and construction of locomotives. By 1944 the work force had risen to 7,500 from 6,500 in 1939, a total which included 1,000 women.

At Nationalisation in 1948, Crewe was building its last two `Coronation´ class Pacifics and was continuing with a batch of 50 `Black Fives´. Unlike the problems which had occurred at the Grouping, Crewe was not out of step at Nationalisation, and when the Standard range of BR steam locomotives had been agreed, it was Crewe that was chosen to build all of the `Pacifics´. The first of these, No 70000 *Britannia*, was outshopped at the beginning of 1951 and, in all, Crewe was to build 289 out of the 999 BR Standards. Between 1951 and 1954, Crewe constructed 55 `Britannias´, 10 `Clans´ and the solitary Class 8 No 71000 *Duke of Gloucester*. Following these were the `9F´ 2-10-0s, of which Crewe built 198 out of a total of 251, the very last steam locomotive being `9F´ No 92250, declared to be the 7,331st since construction had begun. From this date Crewe continued to carry out repairs to steam locomotives until 2 February 1967 when `Britannia´ No 70013 *Oliver Cromwell* left to resume normal service. Becoming part of British Rail Engineering Ltd in 1970, Crewe has continued to produce 25kv electric locomotives and HST power cars in addition to Class 56 diesel locomotives and was privatised as BREL Ltd in April 1989.

Rugby (2A) MPD´s Ex-Works Stanier 2-8-0 No 48131 receives attention from the crew in this picture taken at Willesden in April 1960. No 48131 had entered Crewe on 26 March 1960 for an Intermediate repair. Often host to over 100 engines, some invariably priming the North West London air with coal tar and adding to the gritty fumes from the nearby Acton Lane power station, it was easy to see why Willesden was dubbed `The Old Grey Lady of the London Midland´. *G. Rixon*

Left:
Former Caledonian Railway 0-4-0ST No 56032 is depicted outside Crewe Works on 13 October 1957. This locomotive was brought in when the Ramsbottom 0-4-0STs were withdrawn and was used to move around Works `cabs´ - this ensemble which provided a taxi service through the length of the works was also used for the distribution of wages. *W. Potter*

Left:
A relic which survived at Crewe for many years was the former Ince Wagon Works shunter, seen here outside the Paint Shop on 20 March 1960. *T.B. Owen*

Below:
LMS `Jubilee´ 4-6-0 No 45671 *Prince Rupert*, seen on 20 March 1960, is still in primer as it awaits entry into the Paint Shop following a General repair. A Longsight (9A) locomotive since October 1957, No 45671 saw allocations to Llandudno Junction, Crewe North and Warrington before returning to Crewe Works for breaking in November 1963. *T.B. Owen*

Following repair at Crewe Works, Stanier '8F' 2-8-0 No 48077 is working a Sunday permanent way train at Ridgmont, between Bedford and Bletchley, in July 1965. The steam shed at Bletchley closed on 5 July 1965 and was replaced by a diesel and electric depot alongside the Bedford branch. *R. Hobbs*

Fresh from overhaul at Crewe works, Crosti-boilered '9F' 2-10-0 No 92025 nears Shap summit with a car carrier freight in October 1965. The 10 Crosti 2-10-0s were not an improvement on the original Standard Class 9F design as severe corrosion within the pre-heating barrel led to excessive maintenance costs and the locomotives were rebuilt with conventional exhaust arrangements, although still retaining the Crosti look.

R.Hobbs

Above:
`Britannia´ Pacific No 70013 *Oliver Cromwell* is depicted at Carnforth in August 1968. Whilst No 70013 was the last locomotive to receive a heavy repair in normal service, other locomotives including `A4s´ Nos 60009, 60010 and 4498 were overhauled later in 1967 and 14 years later in 1981, No 46229 *Duchess of Hamilton* arrived for a welding repair. *D. Huntriss*

Below:
A trainspotter's nightmare; `Royal Scot´ 4-6-0 *Royal Scots Grey* arrived at Crewe for an Intermediate repair on 5 March 1960. Here, the frames of 46101 carry the nameplate *Royal Scots Grey* and the smokebox door bears the number 46101. However, the adjacent locomotive, believed to be No 46113 *Cameronian* bears the cab side sheet from 46101. *T.B. Owen*

Left:
`Bissel Truck´ 0-4-2ST No 47862 is seen at Crewe Works between duties on 27 May 1956. Designed by Webb for the LNWR and introduced in 1896, No 47862 was the last member of the class to survive , its final years being spent as a Crewe Works shunter. *T.B. Owen*

Left:
Larger motive power saw use on Crewe Works shunting turns at times, and here on 10 June 1956, Ex-LNWR Webb `18in Goods´ `Cauliflower´ 0-6-0 No 58427 appears to be out of use. Introduced in 1887, No 58427 was one of many class members to be rebuilt with a Belpaire boiler.
T.B. Owen

Below:
Banbury (2D) MPD's `9F´ 2-10-0 No 92030 is seen climbing through Harbury cutting with a mineral train in October 1965. Recently out-shopped from Crewe Works, No 92030 remained operational from Banbury until June 1965, when it was reallocated to Wakefield (56A) MPD.
Derek Huntriss

Left:
LMS `Jubilee´ 4-6-0 No 45700
Amethyst **is seen outside Crewe Works following repair on 18 August 1962. The author can well recall the excitement the appearance of this Newton Heath (26A) MPD engine caused when it arrived in Coventry on a running in turn during the school holidays.** *T.B. Owen*

Above:
Straight from the Paint Shop at Crewe Works, Shrewsbury (89A) MPD's Class 5 4-6-0 No 45422 is seen outside Crewe Station on 22 September 1961. *W. Potter*

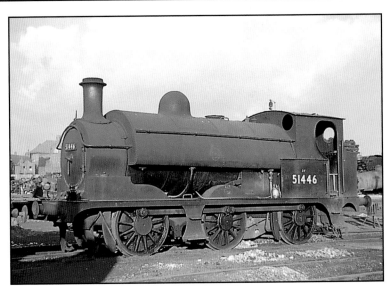

Right:
Carrying the early BR emblem ex-L&Y 0-6-0ST No 51446 is seen between duties outside Crewe Works on 15 March 1959. Introduced in 1891, this class was a rebuild of the L&Y Barton Wright Class 23 0-6-0, originally introduced in 1877. *T.B. Owen*

Above:
Entering traffic in June 1955, Wellingborough (15A) MPD´s Crosti-boilered `9F´ 2-10-0 No 92025 is seen outside Crewe Works on 13 October 1957. All 10 of this type were allocated to Wellingborough up until July 1963, when No 92022 was transferred to Rowsley. *T.B. Owen*

Below:
Observed on the Test Roads at Crewe Works some three weeks earlier on 18 August 1963, Class 5 4-6-0 No 44674 prepares to back down into the smoky environs of Willesden shed yard on 9 September 1963.
G. Rixon

Above:

Penultimate member of the `Princess Royal´ class, No 46211 *Queen Maud* is depicted outside Crewe Works on 15 March 1959. At this time No 46211 had received a Casual repair during which she had undergone a piston and valve exam and had also been fitted with ATC, the small cylindrical aws timing reservoir being visible in front of the cab. The larger aws timing reservoir was situated on the other side of the loco.

Seen in her final condition with domed boiler, 6211 entered traffic in September 1935 and was named after Queen Maud of Norway.

T.B. Owen

Left:

Twilight of steam. BR `9F´ 2-10-0 No 92118 is seen preparing to depart from Banbury (2D) MPD on 18 June 1966, prior to taking a Banbury to Bordesley freight. At this time Ex-works locomotives were few and far between, and in the main their external condition deteriorated rapidly on return to their depot. *D. Huntriss*

Top Right:

This interesting picture taken outside Crewe Works on 10 June 1956 shows contrasts in West Coast freight motive power. In the background is ex-LNWR 0-8-0 No 49094 and in front are the frames and motion of new BR `9F´ 2-10-0 No 92099. *T.B. Owen*

Bottom Right:

Having arrived at Crewe Works for an Intermediate repair on 24 May 1958, Bletchley (1E) MPD´s ex-LNWR 0-8-0 No 48898 is depicted at March (31B) MPD on 23 June 1958. *R.C. Riley*

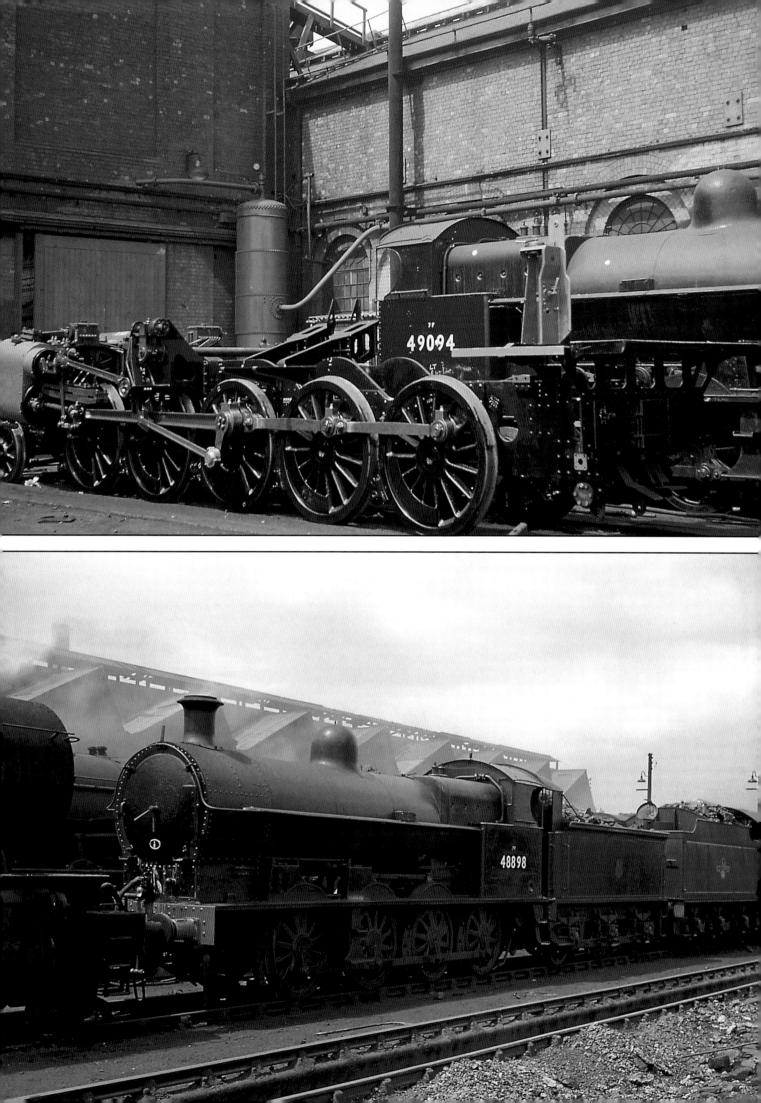

Right:
One of the few occasions on which ex-WD 2-8-0s could be seen in a clean external condition was when they were straight out of shops. Here, Lostock Hall (24C) MPD's No 90266 is depicted outside Crewe Works on 13 October 1957. *W.Potter*

Below:
This superb view taken on 16 April 1961 outside Crewe Works shows a hive of activity. Locomotives under repair include Stanier 2-6-4T No 42662, Pacific No 46254 *City of Stoke-on-Trent* and St Philips Marsh (82B) MPD's Ivatt 2-6-0 No 46525. *W. Potter*

Left:
An excellent detail view taken inside the Frame shop at Crewe Works on 23 February 1958. Both in the foreground and on the left are the frames for new Class 9F 2-10-0s. *W. Potter*

Above:
One activity undertaken at works was the restoration of locomotives for preservation. Here, Stanier LMS Pacific, No 6233 *Duchess of Sutherland*, is seen at Crewe Works on 30 August 1964, prior to being dispatched to Butlin's Heads of Ayr holiday camp. *W. Potter*

Below:
An early example of locomotive preservation was LNWR 2-2-2 No 3020 *Cornwall*, seen here at Crewe in 1958. Originally built by Francis Trevithick in 1847 and rebuilt by Ramsbottom in 1858, No 3020 was used to work Directors' saloons until 1927. *D. Penney*

Midland 'Compound' No 1000 prepares to depart from Birmingham New St with an SLS railtour on 27 September 1959. On 22 March 1959, No 1000 had been observed in the Erecting Shop at Derby where it had required heavy frame repairs including large welded inserts. *A.N.H. Glover*

TEN

DERBY

The Midland Railway Co, formed by Act of Parliament on 10 May 1844, brought together three railway companies which had received the Royal Assent in 1836. The three railways, all terminating at Derby, were the Birmingham & Derby Junction Railway, the Midland Counties Railway and the North Midland Railway. From this date the sheds and workshops of the North Midland and Midland Counties companies now formed the basis of what was to become the Midland Railway's Derby Locomotive Works.

Upon the company's formation Matthew Kirtley became the Locomotive and Carriage Superintendent, and he persuaded the Board that there were inadequate facilities at Derby to meet the requirements of an ever expanding railway. To this end a second roundhouse accommodating 16 locomotives was built in 1847, further workshops and repair facilities were added and by 1851 there was sufficient capacity for new locomotive construction to begin. The first locomotive built was a single-framed 0-6-0 goods engine, No 147, followed by many more new engines in addition to a number of `rebuilds´. A further four-road roundhouse was added in 1852, this expansion continuing into the 1860s with the addition of more mess rooms and more workshops.

Before his death in 1873, Kirtley had masterminded another plan for expanding the building capacity at Derby Works. Prominent in his plans was the separation of the Carriage and Wagon Department, 50 acres of land being set aside for this purpose on the opposite side of the London main line. These structures were in operation by July 1877 under the management of Thomas Clayton, who had been appointed as Carriage and Wagon Superintendent in July 1873.

Upon the death of Matthew Kirtley in May 1873, he was succeeded by Samuel Waite Johnson who was appointed Locomotive Superintendent in July 1873. His task was to reorganise the Locomotive Department of the Midland Railway and to provide better accommodation for his staff and the locomotives right across the system. With the addition of new workshops at Derby many more new locomotives were built, the Midland still having to rely on contractors, but to a lesser degree. By 1890 locomotive accommodation was beginning to prove a problem so a fourth and much larger shed was opened. This rectangular construction comprised two turntables with 22 stabling roads radiating from each. This extra building was necessary because the existing North Midland shed was being used for repair work and the shed of 1847 was being used to house spare engines. Johnson was not a man easily converted to revolutionary ideas, but preferred to wait patiently until such time as developments ensured his success. In particular, this was the case with steam brakes, steam and automatic brake combined and later the train-heating apparatus. This same logic also applied to Johnson's re-introduction of the single driver. No single driver locomotives had been built by the Midland since 1866, but after some unofficial experimentation by the District Locomotive Superintendent at Leicester, Johnson's next batch of five singles was turned out between June and August 1887. These locomotives had driving wheels of 7ft 4in diameter, the largest used on Midland main line locomotives. These were a great success with Johnson embarking on a building programme which continued up until 1900.

Retiring at the end of 1903, Johnson was succeeded by Richard Mountford Deeley, who took office at the beginning of 1904. Unlike his predecessors, Deeley had worked his way up through the ranks. The first locomotives turned out by him were simply further orders and rebuilds of earlier Johnson types with large boilers being fitted to many of the earlier passenger tender engine classes. The year 1905 saw the first of Deeley's modified compounds, this being No 1000, which was turned out in October.

Following Deeley's somewhat controversial resignation in August 1909, Henry Fowler made his entrance as the first CME (and also the last) in January 1910. During World War 1, Derby Works played an important role in the supply of munitions. Work undertaken was the renovation of cartridge cases, Howitzer cradles and numerous other pieces of equipment including special machinery for the Railway Transport Expeditionary Force.

Upon the Grouping in 1923, the London, Midland & Scottish Railway was formed, an organisation which embraced not only the Midland, but also such former rivals as the London & North Western Railway, Lancashire & Yorkshire Railway and the North Staffordshire Railway together with lines in the north and smaller lines in the south. Within this new organisation, Derby Works became an important centre. On 1 January 1923 the LMS took over 10,316 locomotives of no fewer than 393 different types. This led to the development and introduction of 14 standard types which appeared before the appointment of William Arthur Stanier as CME in 1932. Of these, four classes of Midland engine were adopted as standard. These were the compound 4-4-0s, the superheated Class 2 4-4-0s, the 0-6-0 Class 4 tender engines and the 0-6-0 Class 3F tank engines.

With the arrival of Stanier in 1932, there was a turning point in LMS locomotive design. The reign of the Midland's small engine policy had come to an end and to Stanier's great credit, he was to renew almost all of the LMS `first string´ locomotive fleet within the next eight years. Following the surrender of France in World War 2, Derby shops had to be hurriedly reorganised to cope with the increased demand for aircraft components which included new wings for Hurricane and Typhoon fighter aircraft. Later in the war work began on fuselage repairs for Whitley, Hampden and Lancaster bombers, these often coming straight from RAF depots. With the urgent need for additional motive power during the war years, many older locomotives were reprieved and given repairs to prolong their economic life.

On the 1 January 1948, the four main line groups of railways were `Nationalised´, and Derby Works found themselves competing with other works scattered throughout the rest of the British Railways system. By 1952 Derby had turned out its first batch of ten Standard Class 4MT 2-6-4 tank engines, although 5 December 1947 saw Derby's first main line diesel-electric locomotive leave the shops. The production of this locomotive, No 10000, had been a collaborative project between the LMS and English Electric companies. No 10000 made its first run to London on 16 December 1947 and a second unit, No 10001, entered service on 10 July 1948.

Steam locomotive construction ended at Derby in June 1957 when BR Standard Class 5 4-6-0 No 73154 was completed, bringing the total number of steam locomotives built to 2,995. The last steam locomotive to be repaired at Derby, Standard Class 4 4-6-0 No 75042, left the works under its own power on 20 September 1963. By 1967 Derby Works had built their last diesel locomotive, Class 25 No D7677 and by 1988 Classified repairs of diesel locomotives came to an end.

Above:
This superb view, taken at Derby shed on 24 September 1961, depicts Midland `1F´ half-cab 0-6-0T No 41835, prior to its return to Canklow (41D) MPD. Due at Derby Works for a General repair on W/E 11 April 1961, No 41835 was the last member of the class to lose its round top firebox and spring balance safety valves, an operation completed during this visit to works. *R.C. Riley*

Left:
A long way from home, Carnforth (24L) MPD´s `Jinty´ 0-6-0T No 47410 is at Derby MPD on 1 November 1959 following a General repair. *A.N.H. Glover*

Left:
Depicted outside Derby (17A) MPD on 25 September 1955, `Compound´ 4-4-0 No 41083 had been due on Works for an Intermediate repair on 24 August. It remained allocated to Derby until withdrawn from traffic in December 1958. *R.C. Riley*

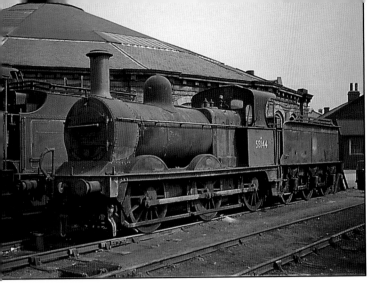

Left:
Paint peeling and going rusty, Johnson Midland 0-6-0 No 58144 has reached its final resting place outside Derby Works on 7 August 1960. A locomotive type seldom photographed in colour, this class of engine, introduced in 1917, was the Johnson 5ft 3in design, rebuilt with Belpaire firebox; the earlier Johnson Midland 4ft 11in design, introduced in 1875, having a round top firebox. *W. Potter*

Left:
Stoke (5D) MPD´s Fowler 2-6-4T No 42400 is seen outside Derby MPD on 11 March 1956 following a General repair at the Works. Built with side-window cab and doors, No 42400 remained allocated to Stoke until July 1958 and during the remainder of its life in operation spent time at Longsight, Stafford and Saltley MPDs. *N. Fields*

Below:
This ex-Works view of LMS `4F´ No 44414 was taken on 30 September 1962 outside Derby MPD. The Class 4F 0-6-0 was the final design of Midland goods engine and although built by the LMS, it looked little different from its Midland predecessors. Apart from its five digit number and BR livery, there are few significant changes from its LMS condition. *Ray Reed*

Above:
**Crewe North (5A) MPD´s Stanier `Coronation´ class Pacific No 46245
City of London is at Derby Works open day on 29 August 1964. No 46245
is carrying the distinctive cab-side yellow stripe denoting that its use
under energised overhead electrified wires was prohibited.** *N. Fields*

Below:
**LMS `2P´ 4-4-0 No 40700 is seen outside Derby Works on 25 August
1962. A group of youngsters attending the open day enjoy the pleasure
of the footplate as they take a break from the long trudge round the
factory.**
G. Rixon

these being No D3593 and the last, No D4157, leaving the works on 28 December 1962.

With the closure of Gorton Works in 1963, Horwich resumed the manufacture of points and crossings. During 1963 the number of locomotives requiring repair declined, the erecting shop being invaded by wagons, many of these as a result of the running down of Earlestown Works. On 6 May 1964, Stanier 2-8-0 No 48756 left Horwich Works after a general overhaul, after which the great works of the former Lancashire & Yorkshire Railway were occupied only with rolling stock and road vehicles. In January 1970 Horwich Works became part of BREL and in 1982 the main works closed leaving only the foundry which was sold as a going concern in 1987.

Today, we only have memories of Horwich and its greatness. Some of the first experiments with superheaters were carried out here by Aspinall and Hughes. Of the famous locomotives designed and built at Horwich were the 2-4-2 `Radial´ tanks, the 4-4-2 `High Flyers´ and the great Hughes 4-6-4Ts, possibly the most impressive tank design locomotive produced in this country. Locomotives that must not be forgotten were the hard-worked `Crab´ 2-6-0s.

Other Horwich products were some of the greatest names in locomotive engineering who were trained there. These include Sir Nigel Gresley, R.E.L. Maunsell, George Hughes and Sir Henry Fowler, J.P. Crouch who became CME of the Argentine Central and Rupert Fawker CME of the Sudanese Railways. As well as all these stood one of the greatest of all railwaymen, Sir John Aspinall.

Nuneaton (2B) MPD´s Stanier '8F' 2-8-0 No 48343 is seen outside Horwich Works following repair on 13 October 1963. Six months later, on 6 May 1964, the last steam locomotive to be repaired, Stanier `8F´ No 48756, left the works, bringing to an end an 80 year association with steam.

K. Fairey

Above:
A splendid view of ex-L&Y 0-6-0ST works shunter No 11324 taken on 13 October 1963. *A.N.H. Glover*

Left:
18in gauge 0-4-ST *Wren* is seen preserved inside Horwich Works on 13 October 1963. The 18in gauge system was built to link the stores with every part of the works and total track mileage amounted to 7½ miles. *Wren* was one of eight 0-4-0ST locomotives built to work the system. *Robin*, *Wren* and *Dot* were built by Beyer Peacock in 1887, and the others were built at Horwich - *Fly* and *Wasp* in 1891, *Midget* and *Mouse* in 1899 and *Bee* in 1901. *A.N.H. Glover*

Left:
Another major activity at locomotive workshops was that of locomotive breaking. Here, Stanier `Crab´ 2-6-0 No 42984 is in the process of being dismantled. Today only one member of this 40 strong class survives in preservation. No 42968 is fully restored and can be seen in operation on the Severn Valley Railway. *A.N.H. Glover*

77

Above:
`The Pride of Sowerby Bridge´, ex-L&Y 0-6-0 No 52515, always kept in ex-Works condition, is depicted at Sowerby Bridge together with LMS `4F´ 0-6-0 No 44408 at the head of the `South Yorkshireman´ railtour on 29 September 1962. *G.W. Morrison*

Below:
Fresh from overhaul at Horwich Works, Fowler `Crab´ 2-6-0 No 42789 is seen outside Farnley Junction (55C) MPD on 1 June 1962. The following month No 42789 was to move to Bradford Manningham (55F) MPD before departing for Ayr (67C) MPD in November 1962. *G.W. Morrison*

Above:
Still to be repatriated with their tenders, LMS `4F´ 0-6-0 No 44065 and Ivatt Class 2 2-6-0 No 43015 are depicted outside Horwich Works on 16 September 1962. *Peter Fitton*

Below:
A general view inside the erecting shop at Horwich on 11 August 1963 shows the frames and cab-side of Stanier `Crab´ No 42955, and, further from the camera, Standard Class 4 2-6-0 No 76020. *W. Potter*

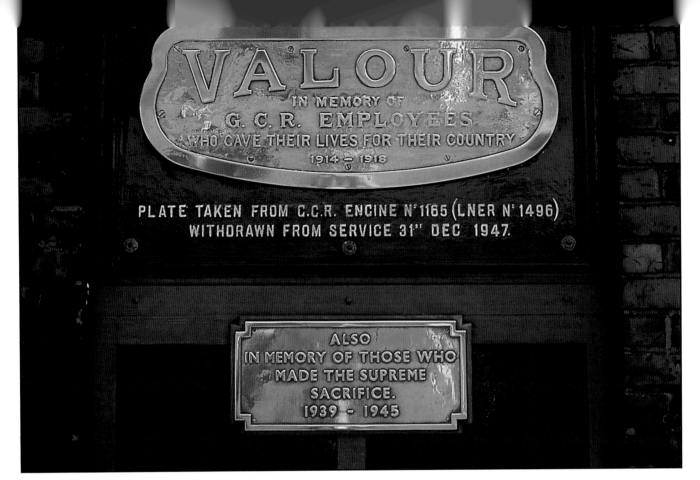

Above:
Dedicated to GCR employees who gave their lives during World War 1, the plate from GCR Class 9P 4-6-0 No 1165 *Valour* hung as a permanent memorial inside Gorton Works. On closure of the works in 1962, the plate was on display in a local church from where it was later stolen. Luckily the plate from the other side is in the NRM. *T.B. Owen*

Below:
This interesting view taken inside Gorton Works on 26 June 1960, shows Class EM1 electrics under repair alongside steam locomotives. Designed by Gresley for the Manchester, Sheffield and Wath electrification scheme, all except the first Bo-Bo which was built by Metropolitan-Vickers, were constructed at Gorton between 1950 and 1953. *T.B. Owen*

TWELVE

GORTON

Constructed for the Manchester, Sheffield & Lincolnshire Railway Co in 1848, the Locomotive Works at Gorton, Manchester covered a total of 30 acres. In their early years the Works were kept too busy with repairs for the construction of new locomotives to be considered and by1854 the motive power requirements of some railways temporarily exceeded the capacity of builders to complete all their orders. At that time the MS&L urgently needed capital to extend its capacity at Gorton so the company decided to sell off five of its newest goods locomotives to raise the necessary funds. During the last six months of 1863 repairs were completed on 103 locomotives, 281 carriages, 2,988 wagons and 2 steamboats and it was not until 1865 that the annual output of new locomotives reached double figures.

Bounding the western side of the site at Gorton were the carriage and wagon shops which were capable of taking 38 carriages on the upper floor and 50 wagons on the ground floor, the former being raised and lowered by a self-acting hoist powered by a stationary engine. Adjacent to these were the trimming and saddlery room and parallelling the main line was the paint shop which also contained accommodation for reserve rolling stock. The four sections used as the locomotive workshops were served by a traverser which also served the carriage and wagon shops.

From 1897 the premises came under the auspices of the Great Central Railway, which in 1899 had begun to operate express passenger services on its newly-opened extension to London. Initially the principal expresses were light, some operating with only four bogie coaches. The GCR´s then Locomotive Superintendent, Harry Pollitt, was succeeded in 1900 by J.G. Robinson, a Great Western Railway trained engineer, who soon realised that more powerful motive power would be needed. In 1901 he introduced the first of his Class 11B 4-4-0s which were similar to Pollitt´s earlier Class 11A, having a slightly longer firebox and larger boiler. These locomotives, becoming Class D9 under the LNER, operated much of the passenger traffic over the former Cheshire Lines Committee routes, for which the GCR, and later the LNER, provided motive power.

The next express passenger locomotive types to emerge from Gorton Works in 1903 were the Robinson Atlantic and 4-6-0 locomotives with outside cylinders and outside slide valves worked by Stephenson´s link motion, as used on all of his locomotives. Both classes gave good results, a further 25 Atlantics being constructed by 1906. Nicknamed `Jersey Lilies´ after a celebrated Edwardian beauty, they were elegant machines in their Brunswick green livery with claret coloured splashers. Four additional Atlantics, this time three-cylinder compounds were built at the end of 1905. These machines, both simple and compound, were for many years the mainstay of passenger working from Leicester motive power depot, where they were used on expresses to London, Sheffield and Manchester.

The next new passenger type to emerge from Gorton was the `Sir Sam Fay´ locomotive, six being constructed between 1912-13. These large inside-cylindered 4-6-0s were powerful and impressive and having 50% more adhesive weight than the Atlantics, they were more at home climbing severe grades with heavy trains. However, not all was well with these machines. The relatively short connecting rods transmitting thrust from their inclined cylinders, resulting in heavy wear on the driving axle-boxes. This problem was later overcome by reducing the diameter of the cylinders from 21$\frac{1}{2}$in to 20in. Another problem encountered on this

class was the limited clearance of only 7in between the bottom of the firegrate and a sleeve which carried the trailing coupled axle where it passed through the ashpan. On continuous long runs this feature meant that part of the ashpan could become blocked with the knock on effect of reducing the area through which air for combustion was drawn.

While the works were still constructing the last of the `Sir Sam Fay´ 4-6-0s, the design department was completing the drawings for the celebrated Class 11E , the `Director´ class 4-4-0s. These superheated 4-4-0s were a shortened version of the `Sir Sam Fay´ type with the boiler diameter reduced by 3in and its length by 5ft. The problems of ashpan blockage were reduced and gave a virtually unrestricted ashpan for the full length of the firegrate. As with all Robinson designed locomotives, the short valve-travel and steam lap with large diameter piston valves and steam ports made the `Directors´ free running. After the Grouping Gresley was so impressed with the performance of the `Directors´ that he ordered a further 24 of the later `D11´ series for use on the former North British routes in Scotland.

To meet the demands of heavy wartime passenger traffic in 1917, Robinson introduced the prototype four-cylinder 4-6-0 Class 9P `Lord Faringdon´. With a maximum tractive effort which was 10% greater than the `Sir Sam Fays´, this was in effect a four-cylinder version of that class. However, the rear ashpan constriction remained, although in the 38 similar 4-6-0 locomotives built between 1921 and 1924 the problem was resolved by reducing the coupled wheels to 5ft 8in, a feature which enabled the clearance over the trailing coupled axle sleeve in a deeper ashpan to be doubled. Five more `Lord Faringdons´ were built in 1920, including the GC Memorial Locomotive *Valour*. (See picture opposite.) These machines did some extremely good work in the 1930s between Marylebone and Leicester on the tightly timed `Newspaper Express´. Between 1929 and 1938, Gresley converted four members of the class to Caprotti poppet valve gear, a feature which greatly reduced their coal consumption.

With the arrival of newer Gresley machines on former GCR lines between 1936 and 1939 many of the Robinson types were displaced from most principal expresses and the arrival of Thompson `B1´ 4-6-0s between 1948 and 1950 marked the end of the GCR Atlantic and 4-6-0 classes. At the time the LNER was formed, Gorton Works had constructed a total of 921 locomotives, which, in addition to the aforementioned classes, included the `A5´ Pacific tanks, `J11´ 0-6-0s, `O4´ 2-8-0s and `N5´ 0-6-2Ts. The last steam locomotive constructed at Gorton was `B1´ class 4-6-0 No 61349 in 1949. This engine brought the total number of locomotives built to 1,006.

During the early 1950s, Gorton had a total workforce of 2,724 who were mainly employed on locomotive repairs and the manufacture of a variety of new parts. In addition to the repair of steam locomotives, Gorton manufactured and assembled the mechanical parts for a total of 64 electric locomotives for the Pennine route from Manchester to Sheffield, via Woodhead Tunnel, electrification of which had been finally completed in 1952. These were the `27XXX´ passenger and `26XXX´ freight locomotives, the last to be constructed, No 27006, leaving the works in 1954. Upon the formation of the BR Workshops Division in 1962 much of Gorton´s workload was transferred to Doncaster and by 1963 the works had closed. In 1965 followed the closure of the Carriage & Wagon works and today a supermarket stands on the site.

Above:
This picture, taken inside Inverurie Works on 7 June 1962, depicts Class J37 No 64606 undergoing a Non-Classified repair. Having arrived at Inverurie on 23 May, St Margarets (64A) MPD's `J37´ left for home on the following day, 8 June 1962. *Hugh Ramsey*

Below:
Thornton Junction (62A) MPD's sister `J37´class, No 64635, is depicted in steam outside Inverurie Works on 13 June 1960. No 64635 was officially booked off works on 3 June after a repair which included the fitting of AWS apparatus. *T.B. Owen*

THIRTEEN

INVERURIE

Serving what is known today as the Grampian Region, the Great North of Scotland Railway was a compact system which radiated north and west from Aberdeen where it formed an end on junction with the Caledonian and North British Railways. The same Grampian mountains which forced connections from the south into the coastal strip formed the southern boundary, and to the west it abutted the Highland Railway. The main line of the GNSR ran from Aberdeen to Elgin via Keith and the coast line, also to Elgin, ran via Portsoy and Buckie.

The first locomotive works of the GNSR was established at Kittybrewster behind the Aberdeen terminus of the line, a decision that was later to prove a mistake. The cramped conditions at this location meant that a good deal of work was being carried out in the open in all weathers, this leading to requests by successive Locomotive Superintendents for more accommodation. While extensions were authorised in 1891, there were clearly second thoughts and work was suspended until the costs of complete removal were investigated. At a Board meeting on 18 May 1892, it was decided that an entirely new works was required. Following investigations both at Dyce and at Souterford Bridge, Inverurie, the latter site was chosen as the location for the new workshops. To establish the exact requirements a committee was formed, its members visiting the Works at Doncaster, Swindon, Wolverhampton, Stratford, Crewe (Loco), Kilmarnock and the Ashbury Carriage Co´s factory at Openshaw.

Having asked advice from Mr Holden (GER) and Mr Dean (GWR), it was the latter gentleman who was consulted to advise on the buildings and machinery necessary to set up the workshops. Work commenced in 1898, the first block being ready for occupation by the Carriage & Wagon Dept some three years later. These were followed in 1902 by the Locomotive Department, the PW Dept arriving in 1905.

When the works was still at the design stage, there were proposals to amalgamate the GNSR with the Highland Railway, and it has been suggested that the spacious layout at Inverurie was designed to accommodate the overhaul of both company´s rolling stock. However, it was to be 1914 before the GNSR agreed to repair Highland Railway locomotives, an agreement which excluded heavy boiler repairs.

The opening of the Works at Inverurie meant an immediate increase in the population, previously estimated to be about 1,200, the company building a number of houses for occupation by their employees. This accommodation consisted of a block for the Locomotive Superintendent with a further four blocks with gardens for the office staff and foremen in addition to five blocks of three and four roomed houses for the workmen. All of these were supplied with electricity from the Works and in addition ground was made available for garden plots and a large park. With the provision of recreation rooms and a hall, a virtually new town had been created and while there was no doubt that this benefited the burgh, it was seen as an expensive luxury by the shareholders.

The locomotive list of the GNSR only ever came to about 180, most of these being constructed by independent locomotive builders, although two were built or assembled at Kittybrewster before the opening of Inverurie Works. Whilst several more were constructed at Inverurie, the main work was repairs. The most common and useful locomotives were the light 4-4-0s and were to be found in many forms; old, new, rebuilt with superheaters, with and without names. In addition to these there were also some 0-6-0Ts, some attractive 0-4-4Ts and four 0-4-2Ts which

were to be found shunting at Aberdeen Docks. The GNSR had experimented with railmotors on their St Combs and Lossiemouth branches, but they were found to be unsatisfactory and were split into open saloons and stationary boilers.

Carriage construction evolved similarly from spartan four and six-wheelers to comfortable corridor bogie stock by the turn of the century; by 1903 the GNSR could provide its own Royal Train. Freight wagons on the GNSR were fairly typical, being light to match the locomotives although goods brake vans were notable being fully enclosed.

Following the amalgamations of 1923, the Works passed into the ownership of the LNER and brought few changes only in that the patterns were moved to Cowlairs after which the Pattern Shop became the Works Canteen. To the LNER the GNSR contributed some 122 locomotives, and despite the fact that three of them were approaching 60 years of working life, no withdrawals were made before 28 June 1926. The first sign of new ownership was on 9 March 1923 when L & NER No 72 was `Ex-Works´, the ampersand continuing to appear for another four months. This practice was discontinued when No 108 left the shops without the ampersand and carrying its own GNSR number but with the suffix S to indicate to which section of the LNER it belonged. The cast brass numberplates of pre-Grouping origin were not disturbed or altered, a style which was continued for a further six months. At a meeting of the LNER Locomotive and Traffic Committee in the last week of January 1924, it was decided to cease the use of the suffix, and apart from the North Eastern stock, to add various thousands to those of other section´s numbers, except for the GNSR which was to take the numbers at the end of the GC section. The result was the addition of 6800 to the original GNSR numbers, this becoming effective when No 6812 was `Ex-Works´ on 19 March 1924. As a result this meant that more than half the Northern Scottish Area locomotive stock went straight from GNSR livery to LNER lettering and augmented numbering.

By the mid-1950s the ability of Inverurie Works to carry out the repair of the heavier postwar locomotives was curtailed by the limited capacity of the existing overhead cranes, the plant´s 60-ton crane having been in operation for 50 years. It was decided that the time had come for a new 100-ton capacity crane and gantry to be installed in the centre bay of the erecting shop and a further 40-ton crane be installed in the north bay, the existing 60-ton crane being altered to comply with modern standards.

By the early 1960s some 550 people were employed at Inverurie, the average weekly output being two locomotives with General or Intermediate repairs and one with Casual repairs while 25 carriages and 125 wagons being attended to. With the arrival of diesel traction the west sides of the Boiler, Erecting and Carriage shops were set aside for their maintenance, this space sufficing for attention to 34 main line and 41 diesel multiple units. A battery electric railcar which saw use on the Deeside line in BR days is currently being restored in Lancashire.

Because of its good geographical location, Inverurie survived the re-organisations of 1962 although BR proposals in 1969 suggested that work at Inverurie be diverted to St Rollox. At that time almost half the town's population was employed at the Works. These proposals were discussed with representatives of the trade unions, the British Railways Board giving six months notice of their proposals, the Works gates closing for the last time at the end of December 1969.

Built by the North British Locomotive Co. for the GNSR in 1920, No 49 *Gordon Highlander* is depicted at Kemnay on the branch from Kintore to Alford, working an RCTS/SLS special on 13 June 1960. Withdrawn from Keith (61C) MPD on 23 June 1958 as BR Class D40, No 62277, she was restored at Inverurie Works. *T.B. Owen*

Posed for the camera, outside Inverurie Works on 13 June 1960, Bathgate (64F) MPD's J36´ 0-6-0 No 65265 is ready for despatch following a Light/Intermediate repair. No 65265 was to remain at Bathgate until withdrawn from traffic in November 1963. *T.B. Owen*

Above:
**BR Class 2F 0-6-0 No 57353 is seen under the coal stage at St Rollox
(65B) MPD on 2 June 1957. This former Caledonian Railway `Standard
Goods´ appears to be ex-Works and in the process of being prepared for
the trip back to Hurlford (67B) MPD.** *T.B. Owen*

Below:
**Carrying the early BR `Lion & Wheel´ emblem, LMS Class 5 4-6-0
No 44704 stands outside St Rollox Works on 31 May 1952. Allocated to
Perth (63A) MPD, No 44704 was still there when withdrawn from traffic
some 14 years later, in September 1966.** *T.B. Owen*

FOURTEEN

ST ROLLOX

The origins of the workshops at St Rollox date back to the Glasgow & Garnkirk Railway which was authorised in 1826 and opened for traffic in 1831. This company had an engine shed on part of the site which is today occupied by British Rail Maintenance Ltd´s Springburn Level 5 Depot. The Glasgow & Garnkirk Railway was sold to the Caledonian Railway in 1846 and in 1848 that company authorised the purchase of land at St Rollox on which their workshops were built. These new workshops were occupied in 1856 when the Caledonian Railway´s workshops at Greenock were abandoned. When Dugald Drummond came to the Caledonian Railway he recommended that all major work should be concentrated at St Rollox, the workshops being re-modelled and enlarged in 1886. In the same year a 4-2-2 was constructed by Neilson & Co for the Edinburgh Exhibition, at the end of which it was taken over by the Caledonian Railway. Although primarily designed by the makers, Dugald Drummond evidently had a hand in it, as it embodied certain of his characteristic features, such as the cab and boiler mountings. It took part in the 1888 Race to Scotland between the West and East Coast routes, when it ran between Carlisle and Edinburgh with a load of four coaches, maintaining a daily average time of 107³/4min for the 100³/4 miles. This included the ascent of Beattock, nine miles of continuous climbing between 1 in 74 and 1 in 88, preceded by a further three miles of 1 in 202. For a number of years after World War 1 it was used only for hauling the Directors´ saloon, but in the early 1930s it was again put into ordinary traffic on local trains between Perth and Dundee, by which time it had received a new boiler, with Ramsbottom safety valves over the firebox instead of mounted in the dome. Withdrawn from traffic in 1935 it remained in store at St Rollox Works until 1958 when it was restored in its Caledonian blue livery with its original No 123.

In 1895 Drummond departed for the LSWR and was succeeded by J.F. McIntosh whose first engines for the Caledonian Railway were the famous `Dunalastair´ class 4-4-0s, which at the time of their appearance were amongst the largest engines in the country. The design was in effect a development of the somewhat similar engines built by Lambie in 1894, which had in turn evolved from those built by Dugald Drummond in 1884. The `Dunalastairs´ themselves were again gradually enlarged, and four distinct varieties, known as the `Dunalastair I, II, III and IV´ classes, appeared between 1895 and 1910. The last engine of the 1910 batch, No 139, was fitted with a superheater and some of the dimensions were modified. It was the first superheated engine in Scotland and one of the first in Great Britain.

In 1901 the International Engineering Congress held its meeting in Glasgow, and members visited the St Rollox workshops of the Caledonian Railway. For the visit the CR produced a brochure giving details of the works, the railway, and recent engines. The following is an extract from that brochure kindly reproduced with permission from the Caledonian Railway Association.

'In 1901 the Caledonian Railway employed 3,130 workmen at St Rollox. The works occupied an area of 24 acres, 13 acres of which was under roofs. The works had been rebuilt in 1882-84 and were planned to facilitate, by a system of 1ft 8¹/2in gauge lines, the passage of material from one department to another during the course of manufacture with a view to economising in labour costs. The works were capable of producing 52 locomotives, 104 carriages, and 3,000 wagons annually.

'The various departments of the works included the Forge, containing five steam hammers, spring bolt and rivet cutting machines, eight furnaces, wheel veeing and spoke bending machines, eight cranes and other ancillary equipment. The Smithy contained eighty hearths, 14 steam hammers, 5 "Olivers", 6 grindstones, polishers and a bending machine. The Spring Shop contained 2 hearths, a furnace, and two hydraulic spring machines. The Boiler Shop equipment included a 25-feet Plate Edging machine, drills for tube plates and boiler barrels, drilling, milling, tapping, punching and shearing machines, a stay cutter, 2 rivetting machines, 8 radial drilling machines, and various cranes, saws and other machinery. The Iron Foundry included two core ovens, 2 cupolas (for melting iron), a core making machine, four molding machines, and a 5-ton overhead travelling crane. Adjoining the Boiler Shop were the pattern-making shop, pattern store, and dressing shop. The Erecting Shop could accommodate 90 locomotives and 20 tenders and contained a portable cylinder boring mill, a double-headed slotting machine for foundation rings, a pneumatic drill, air compressor and air reservoir, and a locomotive weighing machine. The equipment of the Machine Shop included a wide range of drilling, boring, milling, nut-tapping and facing, turning, slotting and planing machines, grinders and an oil extractor. Other shops included the Brass Finishing Shop, the Fitting Shop, The Wheel Shop, the Paint Shop, Carriage and Wagon Shops and the Trimming Shop. The works also had a well equipped sawmill. Within the main works area was a test-house where cast and malleable iron, steel, brass, oils, wagon grease, rubber, timber and other materials used by the Company were tested'.

One of the better known locomotive types built at St Rollox was the `Cardean´ class 4-6-0s, the first two, Nos 49 and 50 being turned out in 1903. At that time they were the most powerful express engines in the country. Five more, Nos 903-7, were constructed in 1906, No 903 bearing the name *Cardean*. No 907 was damaged beyond economic repair in the Quintinshill disaster in 1915. All members of the class lost their names at the Grouping, when they became LMS Nos 14750 and 14751 (Nos 49 and 50), and 14752-55 (Nos 903-6). All were superheated in 1911 but remained virtually unaltered except for the removal of the smokebox wingplates on the first two engines. Nos 14752-5 were scrapped between 1927 and 1930, the original pair lasting until 1932.

In 1927, four years after the Grouping, new construction work ceased at St Rollox and in the same year wagon work was transferred to Barassie and the works were reorganised. Prior to becoming part of the British Transport Commission under Nationalisation in 1948, the number of employees had altered little since the turn of the century with 3,382 members of staff being employed. St Rollox works changed its title again in 1962, becoming part of BR Workshops Division. With the closure of Cowlairs Works in 1968, all repair work was transferred to St Rollox, this being followed by work from Inverurie and Barassie upon their closure. By January 1970 St Rollox became part of British Rail Engineering Ltd, getting the title of Glasgow Works in 1972. Today, St Rollox remains the only main works in Scotland and is currently part of British Rail Maintenance Ltd as Springburn Level 5 Depot.

Top:
**Former Caledonian Railway 0-4-0ST `Pug´ No 56025 is depicted outside
St Rollox Works in May 1959. Having constructed its last locomotive, 0-6-0
No 4476, in 1927, St Rollox became heavily involved in repairs for LMS
locomotives and carriages and during reorganisation in 1968, continued as
the main BR works in Scotland.** *A.N.H. Glover.*

Above:
**Former Caledonian Railway `Standard Goods´ 0-6-0, No 57555, is outside St
Rollox (65B) MPD on 2 June 1957.** *T.B. Owen*

Above:
Kept in store at St Rollox Works from 1934 until 1959, Former HR `Jones Goods´ No 103 is back on home territory at Inverness (60A) MPD on 24 April 1962. *A.N.H. Glover*

Below:
Caledonian Railway 4-2-2 No 123 is depicted at Callander on 10 October 1964. Stored at St Rollox Works from 1935 until 1958, No 123 was overhauled and repainted in Caledonian blue livery. *A.N.H. Glover*

Top:
Haymarket (64B) MPD´s Class B1 4-6-0 No 61076 tops Cowlairs incline in fine form on 11 August 1960. No 61076 left Cowlairs Works only five days earlier where it was fitted with modified bogie springs during a General repair. No 61076 remained allocated to Haymarket until September 1962 when it was transferred to St Margarets (64A) MPD where it stayed until withdrawn in September 1965. *G.W. Morrison*

Above:
Previously observed under repair at Cowlairs Works on 4 April 1966, Fowler `Crab´ 2-6-0 No 42919 heads back to Ayr with a loaded coal train from Killoch colliery on 3 May 1966. By the end of 1965, only 27 of this class remained in traffic and these were allocated to Ayr (67C) and Hurlford (67B) MPD´s on the Scottish Region and to Birkenhead (8H) and Stockport (9B)MPDs on the LM Region. *R. Hobbs*

FIFTEEN

COWLAIRS

In common with many of the early railway companies, the North British Railway started as quite a small concern. Initially with a line from Edinburgh to Berwick, it commenced operations in July 1846. From that time, by a continuous process of expansion, take over, and amalgamations with other companies it was the largest railway system in Scotland until the late 1870s when it reached the apex of its growth. It remained in this position until the 1923 Grouping, when it became the second largest constituent of the newly formed LNER.

Based largely in the central (Glasgow-Edinburgh) belt of Scotland, it had an extensive railway system in the Lothians, a monopoly in Fife, and extended its tentacles as far as Mallaig in the north-west, Aberdeen in the northeast, Silloth in Cumberland to the southwest and Newcastle in the southeast. Its main constituent companies were the Edinburgh, Perth & Dundee Railway, the Monklands Railway and the Edinburgh & Glasgow Railway, which, together with some of the smaller companies, made contributions of locomotive stock to the parent company.

The first locomotive works of the NBR were at St Margarets, Edinburgh, the EP&DR at Burntisland in Fife and those of the E&GR at Cowlairs, Glasgow. It was to the latter that the NBR moved its mainshops, and they became the building works for the system. This remained so throughout its independent NBR life, although some locomotives were `contracted out´ in the earlier days, this trend increased as the demand for locomotives outstripped capacity around the turn of the century. There was a total of 893 locomotives produced during its existence, some 24 of these being for its original E&GR owners. The last locomotives to be built were 20 Reid Class `N15´ 0-6-2Ts built in 1923-4 for the LNER. The vast majority of the balance of locomotives built for the NBR were built by a trio of Glasgow builders, Neilson & Co, Sharp-Stewart & Co and Dubs & Co, who amalgamated in the early 1900s to form the North British Locomotive Company Ltd, this company having no connection with the North British Railway Co other than on a supplier-customer basis. In its various guises it supplied no fewer than 437 locomotives to the NBR and had also supplied locomotives to many of the NBR constituents, 63 of which survived to become NBR property on take over.

Cowlairs continued to build locomotives of NBR design until 1924 when the last engine, Class N15 0-6-2T No 9227, was completed. By coincidence, the shops, which had started new construction when Paton´s six-coupled banking tank *Hercules* was put in hand during 1843, ceased production just over 80 years later with another six-coupled tank which had also been designed for work on Cowlairs bank. Under the LNER Doncaster became the source of inspiration for all new designs, and Cowlairs suffered the fate, which, years before, had been the lot of St Margarets and Burntisland.

At the end of 1918 the NBR stock included a number of units, which, in normal times, would have already been replaced. Furthermore there were serious arrears in maintenance. As a result, when the company was merged into the LNER, there were many duplicate list engines still running which had been kept at work as stop gaps during the preceding difficult period, and which, almost immediately, had to be replaced. The passing of the Railways Act of 1920 had put an end to plans for producing new Cowlairs designs, so that even the latest engines were all of types introduced in or before 1915. Within a few years of the Grouping it was necessary to take steps to replace the ageing `D25´, `D26´, `D27´,

`D28´, `D35´, `D50´, `D51´, `E7´, `G7´, `G8´, `J31´, `J32´, `J33´, `J34´ and `J82´ classes, many engines being consigned to the scrap heap almost immediately. With the demand for smaller locomotives greater in Scotland than in England a number of transfers took place of the older engines from the English constituent companies of the LNER to ex-North British depots to take the place of the condemned Wheatley and Drummond machines. From the North Eastern area came some of the Wilson Wordsell, LNER Class J24 0-6-0s and, from the Great Central, some engines of a similar age in the form of LNER Class J9 0-6-0s. Once established in Scotland, engines of the latter class lost their chimneys, receiving the standard Cowlairs´ pattern in exchange. However, it was not too long before engines of both types found their way to the Cowlairs´ scrap heap. For shunting duties a few North Eastern type and some Great Eastern 0-6-0 tanks came north in addition to several new `J50´ class heavy shunting locomotives, originally a Great Northern design which had been adopted as an LNER standard. `Foreign´ passenger tanks were at first represented by two varieties of 2-4-2 from the Great Eastern, some of which migrated further north to the GNSR section. The English engines transferred from the south were all constructed with the driver´s position on the right-hand side of the footplate, this arrangement being at odds with North British practice, for on Cowlairs´ engines since the days of Beyer Peacock singles, the driver had had his place on the left-hand side.

The more important main line services required new locomotives, but because of the weight restrictions on the Aberdeen road, the largest modern engines were precluded. Consequently the first passenger engines to be supplied was a batch of 24 J.G. Robinson´ second series of `Director´, LNER Class D11, 12 being built by Kitson and 12 by Armstrong Whitworth. When delivered they were unnamed, but before long they received names from Scott´s characters, and from then they were received into the family. A few Gresley´ Class A1 Pacifics were allocated to the North British section, but these were only permitted to work on the Edinburgh-Glasgow route and southwards to Berwick and beyond.

In the early 1930s the weight restrictions over the Aberdeen road were lifted, both the earlier Class A1 and later Class A3 Pacifics being used. This sounded the death knell for the North British Atlantics. The first to be scrapped went in 1933 and the remainder of the class followed within the next four years. The use of Pacifics was only a stepping stone on the way to the introduction of a special class, the Gresley `P2´ 2-8-2s, which were introduced in 1934. The use of an eight-coupled locomotive for express passenger duties was an innovation in this country. The first locomotive, No 2001, was sent to the testing plant at Vitry, near Paris. The information gained from these tests gave rise to modifications which were made to a subsequent batch of four additional engines, these being given a new type of smokebox contour giving a semi-streamlined effect.

By 1947 the workshops at Cowlairs employed some 2,475 staff, a figure which was reduced to 1,260 in 1949, when much of the work had been transferred to Horwich after Nationalisation. In 1962, Cowlairs became part of BR Workshops Division, although by 1968, the works had closed, all remaining activities being carried out at St Rollox Works.

Ex-Works 'A4' No 60015 *Quicksilver* is depicted at Grantham in June 1959 following a General repair at Doncaster Works. *Quicksilver* had an earlier association with Grantham in June 1944 when, together with No 2509 *Silver Link* they were removed from King's Cross when the Germans attacked London with flying bombs. *D. Penney*

SIXTEEN

DONCASTER

Having persuaded the Great Northern Railway to make the route of their main line from London to York through Doncaster, Member of Parliament, Edmund Beckett Denison, was also successful in persuading the GNR board to transfer their main Locomotive Repair Works from Boston to Doncaster. Doncaster was favoured by the board because of its close proximity to large coalfields and centres of iron founding in addition to its having good water communications. Constructed by the Liverpool firm of G. & A. Holme, the works were ready for the Locomotive Superintendent, Archibald Sturrock, and nine of his staff to move to Doncaster in autumn 1852, the move from Boston being completed one year later. Sturrock used outside contractors to supply locomotives to the GNR until 1866 when he was succeeded by Patrick Stirling. With his appointment the GNR adopted a policy of constructing their own locomotives at `The Plant´ as it later became known. As if in anticipation of this change of policy, the erecting shop was enlarged providing 12 more pits to erect and repair locomotives.

Stirling´s first locomotive appeared in the form of an 0-4-2 in 1867. One of his finest designs was his 4-2-2 express passenger engine which became known as `Singles´ or `Eight-Footers´. Displaying many of Stirling´s design characteristics they were domeless because the regulator was fitted in the smokebox, and other features included a brass vertical column cover over Salter spring balance safety valves. A total of 53 `Singles´ were built at Doncaster and during the mid-1890s they were involved in the `Race to the North´ when they were known as `Highflyers´.

Dying suddenly in office in 1895, Stirling was succeeded by Henry A. Ivatt who had previously occupied the position of District Locomotive Superintendent of the Southern Division of the GS&W at Cork. Challenged with the task of providing more powerful locomotives to meet the rapidly increasing goods traffic and heavier passenger trains, Ivatt designed 10 different types of locomotive during his 15-year term of office. His most notable design was the 4-4-2 Atlantic express passenger locomotive, the first of these constructed in 1898 being No 990 *Henry Oakley,* named after the former GNR general manager. Such was its success in extensive trials held over the next two years another 21 such locomotives were built between 1898-1903.

Ivatt retired from the GNR in the autumn of 1911 and was replaced by Nigel Gresley who had been at Doncaster as Carriage and Wagon Superintendent since 1905. Having trained at Crewe he had also worked at Horwich, Blackpool and Newton Heath before arriving at Doncaster. He subsequently went on to design some of the most outstanding steam locomotives ever seen. The first of these (later LNER Class K1) was a 2-6-0 or `Mogul´ built in 1912. Featuring the Walschaerts valve gear this type of engine was produced to meet the GNR´s need for a mixed traffic locomotive, nine more being built in 1913. In an attempt to produce more efficient and powerful locomotives Gresley experimented with multi-cylinder engines, the first of these appearing as a three cylinder 2-8-0 mineral locomotive in 1918. In addition to the unusual choice of using three cylinders, there was the derived gear for actuating the inside cylinder from the two sets of `outside´ Walschaerts gear. This feature was later employed is his 1920 designed `K3´ 2-6-0 locomotive. In place of the rocking shaft previously employed in the 1913 2-6-0, he introduced a simplified conjugated gear in the form of 2:1 ratio rocking levers to work the inside valve.

Gresley´s next major achievement was the introduction of his `A1´ Class Pacific No 1470 which appeared from the `Plant´ in 1922. The second member of this class, No 1471, carried out a test run on 3 September 1922 when it hauled a train consisting of 20 vehicles and weighing 610 tons from King´s Cross to Grantham, a distance of 105.5 miles, in 122 minutes. This was even more remarkable in that the locomotive was hauling 100 tons more than had ever been attempted on the northbound run from King´s Cross. This locomotive was to be the pinnacle of GNR locomotive design in that in 1923 the GNR amalgamated with several other companies to become the LNER.

In a series of further tests on the `A1´ during the late 1920s it was decided to raise the boiler pressure from 180 lb/sq in to 222 lbs/sq in, all new Pacifics leaving the plant having this modification being re-classified as `A3s´. The peak of Pacific locomotive design was probably reached between 1935 and 1938 when Gresley introduced the `A4´ class Pacifics to operate high speed services between King´s Cross and Newcastle. The first of this class to emerge from the `Plant´ was No 2509 *Silver Link* which was regarded at the time as unusual in that the smokebox, boiler, cylinders, running boards and chimney were enveloped in a stream line casing. On a trial run on 27 September 1935 No 2509 reached a speed of 112.5 miles per hour whilst for a distance of 43 miles it averaged over 100mph. This was to be surpassed three years later on 3 July 1938, when No 4468 *Mallard* hauled a test train of 240 tons down Stoke bank at a speed of 126mph, thus establishing what still is the world speed record for steam traction. Before his death in 1941 Gresley had departed from steam locomotive design with a drawing of a Bo-Bo electric locomotive intended for use over the Manchester-Sheffield-Wath electrification scheme. This locomotive was constructed in 1941 although it was then placed in store for the duration of the war.

The successor to Gresley as CME was Edward Thompson whose work was limited in scope owing to the war years, the `Plant´ being heavily engaged in armaments work although due to the urgent need for a mixed traffic engine, 50 LMS designed `8F´ 2-8-0s were built between 1943-1946. Whilst having limited success with reorganisations at the `Plant´, Thompson instigated some rebuilding of his predecessor´s locomotives, so angering not only the workforce, but the railway world in general. Despite the controversy regarding his rebuilds, he arguably produced designs of his own which were the `B1´ class 4-6-0, `L1´ and `A2/3´.

Retiring in 1946, Thompson was succeeded by Arthur Henry Peppercorn, the last person to hold the post of CME of the LNER. He was a great admirer of Gresley design principles, these appearing on his Class A2 locomotive which appeared in 1947. The success of the `A2´ locomotive led Peppercorn to design an `A1´ class Pacific, the first batch of this type not appearing until after nationalisation in 1948. Retiring in 1949 after producing only a small number of new locomotive classes, his `A1´ engine was considered to be the most reliable Pacific ever built.

After Nationalisation, individual locomotive works were controlled by R.A. Riddles, Member of the Railway Executive for Mechanical and Electrical Engineering. Under his auspices, using selected practices from each of the locomotive shops, work on 12 Standard designs was begun in 1949, Doncaster producing Class 4 2-6-0s, Class 5 4-6-0s and 2-6-4Ts between 1952 and 1957. Today Doncaster operates as a Level 5 depot as part of BREL.

Top:
Observed at Doncaster Works undergoing a Heavy repair on 12April 1959, `Britannia´ Pacific No 70013 *Oliver Cromwell* has returned to traffic and is depicted at Doncaster (36A) MPD on 10 May1959. *W. Potter*

Above:
New England MPD´s `B1´ No 61074 is seen on Grantham (34F) MPD following a visit to Doncaster Works in June 1959. No 61074 remained allocated to New England until withdrawn in September 1963. *D. Penney*

Top:
Recently ex-Works Class O4/8 No 63688 is seen outside Retford (36E) MPD in May 1962. This derivation of Class O4 was introduced in 1944 when they were rebuilt with 100A (B1) boilers. *D. Penney*

Above:
A late variation of Class O2 is represented by No 63943, seen running light engine south of Grantham in August 1962. This derivative of Class O2 had the GN-type cab with LNER flared-top standard tender in place of the older 3,500 gallon GNR type. *D. Penney*

Some eight months after undergoing a general repair at Doncaster Works 'A3' No 60055 *Woolwinder* is still in fine external condition on 28 February 1959 as she heads an up express near Brookman's Park. No 60055 was condemned on 4 September 1961 whilst awaiting repair at Doncaster Works.

T.B. Owen

March (31B) MPD's `K3' 2-6-0 No 61826 is ex-Works at Doncaster Carr (36A) MPD on 20 April 1958. Whilst the first 10 `K3s' were fitted with GNR tenders with double coal rails, the remainder had LNER tenders of two patterns - flush-sided or an earlier design with a built out top. *W.Potter*

Six days after leaving the `Plant´
where it had received its final
General repair, `A4´ No 60034
Lord Faringdon is seen at Beeston
with a running-in turn on 6 June
1962. One final change of detail to
No 60034 was the fitting of a
replacement numberplate in
March 1963, this having the true
Gill Sans 6. *G.W. Morrison*

Above:
Class A1 No 60128 *Bongrace* is seen outside Doncaster (36A) MPD on
29 September 1962 following what was to be its last General repair.
During this repair, *Bongrace* was fitted with the boiler previously
used by sister Class A1 No 60146 *Peregrine. G.W. Morrison*

Left:
Also at Doncaster Carr MPD, Class A2/3 No 60522 *Straight Deal*
awaits its first turn of duty following a General repair on 6 March
1960. Having been allocated to York (50A) MPD since 30 May 1948,
No 60522 was transferred to Aberdeen Ferryhill (61B) MPD on 2
December 1962, leaving only one month later for St Margarets (64A)
MPD.
G.W. Morrison

Above:
Class A3 No 60103 *Flying Scotsman* is shown south of Grantham in June 1962 only days after receiving its last (General) repair at 'The Plant'. Less than six months later, on 15 January 1963, *Flying Scotsman* was withdrawn from BR service and bought by Mr A.F. Pegler. Thirty years later No 60103 has returned to its BR guise. *P.J. Hughes/Colour-Rail*

Below:
This view, taken inside the Crimpsall Erecting Shop at Doncaster Works on 20 April 1958, features locomotives undergoing Heavy repair. Gresley Class J6 0-6-0 No 64208 is a visitor from Ardsley (56B) MPD and Class K1 No 62070 will be re-allocated from March (31B) MPD to Stratford (30A) MPD when it leaves `The Plant´ *W.Potter*

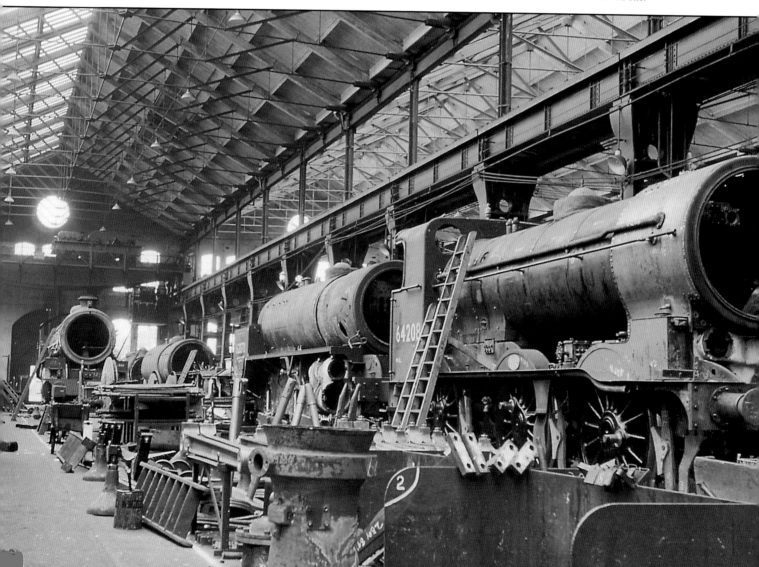

Above:
Staveley GC (41H) MPD's Class O1 No 63630 is Ex-Works at Doncaster MPD following a General repair in October 1960. The Great Central Railway Class O4s and their sister Class O1s, rebuilt by Thompson in 1944, were exclusively designed for use on freight traffic, and the majority, nearly 400, carried out duties on their home territories of Yorkshire, Lincolnshire and Nottinghamshire. *D. Penney*

Above:
This view, taken inside Crimpsall Erecting Shop at Doncaster Works in December 1962, depicts Class A4 No 60004 *William Whitelaw* and Class A3 No 60087 *Blenheim*, both locomotives undergoing a General repair. This was to be their last visit to 'The Plant', although No 60004 had further repairs at Darlington and Inverurie. *D. Penney*

Below:
The bitter end. Entering traffic on 20 July 1939, Gresley Class V2 2-6-0 No 60867 has returned to Doncaster and is in the process of being cut up on 6 May 1962. This locomotive, allocated to Doncaster MPD when new, was transferred to New England MPD on 28 August 1955 where she remained active until withdrawn on 1 May 1962. *Hugh Ramsey*

Following a full repaint, Class Q7 0-8-0 No 63460 heads the RCTS/SLS 'North Eastern Tour' south of Broncepeth on 28 September 1963. Fortunately, No 63460 survives in preservation and currently operates on the North Yorkshire Moors Railway.

T.B. Owen

SEVENTEEN

DARLINGTON

One of Britain´s premier locomotive workshops, Darlington North Road was opened by the Stockton & Darlington Railway and was subsequently owned by the NER, LNER and BR. Today, all that remains is the Locomotive Works clock, mounted on the wall of a supermarket erected on the site in 1980 - 14 years after after the Works closed.

When the Stockton & Darlington line was formally opened in 1825, the locomotive headquarters was at Shildon where Timothy Hackworth struggled to keep the primitive machines in working order. By the 1850s the workshops developed by Hackworth could not manage to keep pace with the locomotives needing repair. In 1854 consideration was given to the future location of improved facilities and by the end of 1857 the necessary land at Darlington had been acquired, plans being prepared by William Bouch, the company´s Engineer and Locomotive Superintendent, in 1858.

After many visits to various locomotive workshops, Bouch estimated that by 1891 the Works would need a staff of 1,300 men and would occupy a space of approximately 16 acres. Work commenced on the site in 1860, the offices and workshops being ready for occupation on 1 January 1863, the final cost of land, buildings, offices and machinery being £34,651 1s 8d. After eighteen months 278 were employed on the site, this figure rising to 339 after a further year. In the 1890s the figure remained constant at around 1,400, a number not too far from Bouch´s estimate. Within a few months of opening, from 13 July 1863, the Stockton & Darlington Railway was taken over by its larger neighbour, the North Eastern Railway, the latter becoming part of the London & North Eastern Railway in 1923.

The first locomotive built at Darlington North Road Works was a short wheelbase 0-6-0 turned out in October 1864 with the number 175 and the name *Contractor*. One of a type favoured by Bouch, engines of a similar design continued to be built until 1875, although attention had turned to 4-4-0 engines in 1871 when Nos 1238-1241 were built, these being followed by Nos 1265-1270 in 1874. Another new design which appeared in 1875 was a 2-4-0 passenger engine of which six were built, the last Bouch design being a batch of four six-coupled side-tanks - an unusual type for the northeast where saddle-tanks were more often found. Between 1871 and 1880, North Road Works built 25 `BTP´ 0-4-4 well tanks to a design by Edward Fletcher (Bouch´s successor), these being followed in 1877 by four Class 11 2-4-0s. Other designs by Fletcher included standard inside framed 0-6-0s of Class 603 and a six-coupled version of his earlier `BTP´ well-tanks.

Retiring in 1882, Edward Fletcher was succeeded by Alexander McDonnell whose first engines were neat 0-6-0s known as Class 59, their design including a smokebox with a sloping front and the unpopular left-hand drive, a type which lasted well into LNER days. With the departure of McDonnell there was an urgent need for express passenger motive power and this need was addressed by the formation of a committee under the chairmanship of Harry Tennant, the General Manager. This committee supervised the construction of 20 engines, 10 being built at Gateshead and 10 at North Road, which were a great success although they were soon displaced by locomotives introduced by T.W. Worsdell, the new Locomotive Superintendent. Worsdell introduced standards which were to serve the North Eastern Railway for the rest of its days - notably double-window cabs on tender engines, closed domes, and Ramsbottom safety valves enclosed in a brass trumpet. At this time, the older Locomotive Works at Gateshead built the most important engines, North Road being left to build only the smaller types, a situation which existed until 1904 when the first large boilered 0-6-0 appeared. These locomotives classified as `P2´ were followed in 1906 by the generally similar Class P3 (LNER Class J27), Darlington building all 35. The first 0-8-0s introduced on the NER were built at Gateshead in 1901 and it was not until 1907 that North Road built the first of 40 Class T1 (LNER Class Q5) engines.

With the run down of Gateshead Works in 1908, North Road built its first large passenger locomotive, the Class R1 (LNER Class D21), not particularly successful, they were followed by ten modified two-cylinder Atlantics which later became LNER Class C6. In 1913, the first of 70 Class T2 (LNER Q6) were turned out, followed in 1919 by the massive Class T3 (LNER Q7) 0-8-0s, the latter remaining in operation until 1962.

Under the superintendency of Raven, 20 large three-cylinder 4-6-2Ts were built of 1910/11, a reversion to two-cylinder propulsion being made with the 20 Class S2 (LNER `B15´) engines, the last locomotives in this series having Uniflow cylinders. Other designs including 35 three-cylinder 4-4-4Ts followed, but it was Raven's Pacifics, the first of which, No 2400, appearing in 1922, that were to be the NER´s magnum opus. However, these were to be relatively short-lived, being eventually overshadowed by the Gresley engines of the same wheel arrangement.

At the Grouping in 1923, `B16´ 4-6-0s were under construction at North Road Works, being closely followed by a batch of five `Y7´ 0-4-0Ts. Concurrently superheated `J27´ 0-6-0s were in hand in addition to three more Raven Pacifics which appeared in 1924. Except for five `T1´ 4-8-0s, Darlington turned to building locomotives of Gresley design, the first of 60 `K3´ 2-6-0s being outshopped in August 1924. Very similar to the 10 locomotives of the same class built at Doncaster, the fitting of a double-window cab considerably altered their appearance. Other classes produced at Darlington at that time included the `J38´ and `J39´ Class 0-6-0s, but 1926 was the year which saw Darlington´s busiest period in LNER days when a total of 52 new engines were constructed - an annual figure not exceeded until the 1950s when 0-6-0 diesel shunters were being built in quantity. Darlington´s first Gresley passenger engine was built in 1927 in the form of `D49´ 4-4-0 No 234 *Yorkshire,* (those intended for use in England were named after the English counties).

In 1929 the unusual `W1´ 4-6-4 was being built at North Road, the boiler being constructed and fitted by Yarrow & Co, the Clydeside shipbuilders. Built under much secrecy it was to be become known as the `Hush-Hush´, its most unusual feature being its water tube boiler. 1930s locomotive construction saw the appearance of a total of 23 `B17´ 4-6-0s on which work began after the design of the first 10, built by the North British Locomotive Co, had been proven. Two new classes which appeared in 1937 were the `V2´ 2-6-2 and the `V4´ 2-6-0s.

The years of World War 2 saw Darlington Works involved in the manufacture of 18-pounder shrapnel shells along with a variety pf bombs. Also during the war `8F´ 2-8-0s were built at Darlington. After the war other classes built were `L1´ 2-6-4Ts and 12 Peppercorn Pacifics, LMS pattern `4MT´ 2-6-0s, LMS and BR `2MT´ 2-6-0s, BR 2-6-2Ts, the last of which was built in 1957. The works closed in 1966.

Top:
Having left Doncaster Works on 5 June 1963 after a General repair, Class K1 2-6-0 No 62027 is depicted at Consett with the RCTS/SLS `North Eastern Tour´ on 28 September 1963. No 62027 was one of the last 24 members of the class to survive into 1967 and was withdrawn from West Hartlepool MPD in September of that year. *T.B. Owen*

Above:
Aberdeen Ferryhill (61B) MPD´s `A4´ No 60019 *Bittern* is seen outside Darlington (51A) shed on 10 April 1965 following a Heavy Intermediate repair at the works. Further repairs were undertaken in Scotland when No 60019 visited Inverurie for a Non-Classified in May 1965 and Cowlairs for a Casual Light in April 1966. *P.J. Fitton*

Above:
In stark contrast to its grubby classmate No 90725, Sutton Oak (8G) MPD´s ex-WD 2-8-0 No 90178 is not long out of shops as it stands outside Wakefield (56A) MPD on 27 October 1962. *J.D. Gomersall*

Below:
Outshopped from Darlington Works only nine days earlier following a General repair, `V2´ No 60913 is seen at Darlington MPD on 12 March 1962. During this repair a Smith speedometer was fitted. *G.W. Morrison*

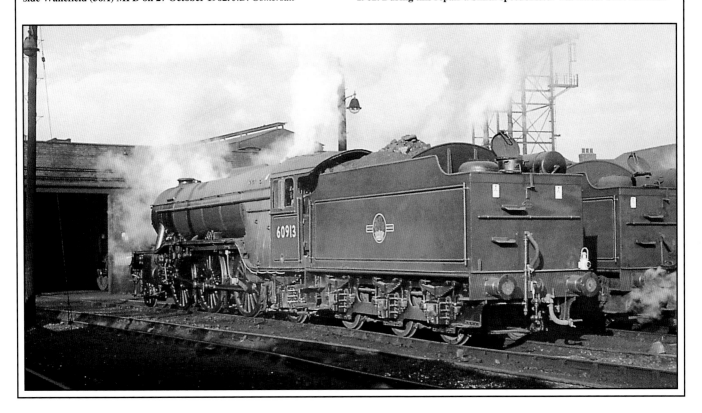

Photographed at Darlington (51A) MPD on 10 April 1965, Class K1 2-6-0 No 62007 has recently undergone a Non-Classified repair, although she had visited Darlington Works only one month earlier for a Heavy Intermediate repair. Surviving until 1967, No 62007 was withdrawn from Tyne Dock (52H) in September of that year. Fortunately, classmate No 62005 survives in preservation. *P.J. Fitton*

Ardsley (56B) MPD's Class B1 4-6-0 No 61013 *Topi* is seen recently outshopped at Darlington MPD on 13 May 1962. Withdrawals of the class began in late 1961 with the loss of No 61085, although No 61013 survived until December 1966 when withdrawn from Wakefield (56A) MPD. *T.B. Owen*

Above:
This interesting view taken inside Darlington Works on 19 September 1965 features the now preserved 'Q6' 0-8-0 No 63395 undergoing Heavy repair. At that time No 63395 was allocated to Sunderland (52G) MPD and saw periods in store at Sunderland, Tyne Dock (52H) and Thornaby (51L) MPDs before restoration. *Hugh Ballantyne*

Below:
York (50A) MPD's Class B16 4-6-0 No 61438 appears in splendid external condition following a General repair when seen at Darlington MPD on 11 October 1961. These handsome 4-6-0s were the last examples of the Raven designed passenger engine to survive into the latter days of steam, although by 1957 they were mainly used for freight. *G.W. Morrison*

This superb portrait, taken outside Stratford Works on 23 March 1958 shows the handsome lines of the Gresley rebuilt 'B12/3' 4-6-0s, of which No 61535 is a superb example. It had emerged from the works on the previous day following a General repair. *T.B. Owen*

EIGHTEEN

STRATFORD

Established in 1847-8, the railway workshops at Stratford were opened when the Eastern Counties Railway´s facilities were unable to expand on their first site at Romford. The Eastern Counties Railway was the first to operate in East Anglia, the first section of line from Mile End to Romford opening in 1839. With the intention of reaching Norwich, the next extension from the City terminus to Brentwood followed shortly afterwards. In 1840 the Northern & Eastern Railway opened with the aim of linking London and Cambridge. Their trains ran over the ECR tracks to Stratford where they followed the Lea Valley northward. At that early date Stratford had become an important railway junction. Having either built, leased or purchased all other railways in East Anglia by the early 1860s, the ECR was re-formed into the Great Eastern Railway.

The original shops which formed the hub of Stratford Works were built by the railway `King´, George Hudson, in the time of the Eastern Counties Railway. In addition to the engineering facilities, Hudson provided accommodation for the workmen in Stratford New Town, an area known for many years as `Hudson´s Town´. The growth of traffic and periodic modernisation of the plant demanded many extensions of the premises and the geography of the works became somewhat complex. The first locomotive was constructed on the site in 1851, and in December 1891 an 0-6-0 tender locomotive was built and steamed in 9hr 47 min, a world record yet to be beaten. By the early 1920s the works at Stratford were one of the most comprehensive railway complexes in Britain. At the hub of the suburban railway system and principal depot for the GER, it was the largest operation of its type in the country. The Engine Repairing Shop was built during World War 1 and adjoined the Running Sheds where plenty of ground was available for extensions. During this war the shops were lent to the Ministry of Munitions and used for the sorting and breaking of steel billets for the manufacture of shell forgings. At that time the Great Eastern´s locomotive fleet consisted of 2-4-0, 4-4-0 and 4-6-0 classes of Passenger tender engines with four types of 0-6-0 goods tender engines and seven types of passenger tank engines. In addition to these there were four classes of goods tank engines for shunting, dock work and local goods traffic.

Having invested heavily on improvements at Stratford Works, it was unfortunate that the Great Eastern Railway had only about four years worth of engine repairs before they became part of the London & North Eastern Railway. The last steam locomotive to be built at Stratford was Class N7 0-6-2T No 999, a locomotive which survives today in preservation. Under LNER ownership, Stratford became the main works for the whole of East Anglia, the lack of new locomotive construction being compensated for by the increase in repair and maintenance work. During the inter war years there were only minor additions and alterations to the workshops although the LNER was progressive in its provision of theoretical training for the apprentices. There were evening classes which were backed up by two afternoon classes during the week designed to prepare apprentices for the National Certificate. The lecturers were draughtsmen and engineers from the works, who were continuing a tradition that was established by the Great Eastern Railway.

In 1939, the railway workshops of Britain were once again involved in a war and the Works at Stratford were no exception. In addition to committing production resources to the war effort, it also had to contend with `The Blitz´. Being situated in close proximity to the docks in the East End of London, the shops took a severe hammering, the old works suf-

fering the brunt of the damage. While the more recent Engine Repair Shop sustained only minor damage, the outside offices at the London end of the shop were destroyed by an incendiary bomb. The ERS suffered damage later in the war when a V2 rocket fell near the High Meads paint shop.

By 1947 there were 2,032 members of staff employed at the works and in 1948 came Nationalisation when Stratford became part of the Eastern Region of British Railways. With the onset of BR´s 1955 Modernisation programme, East Anglia was selected to be the first area to eliminate steam traction completely and rely entirely upon diesel locomotives and multiple unit trains for local and long distance services. For the steam locomotives that remained operational, repairs were transferred to other workshops and Stratford´s Engine Repair shop was converted for diesel locomotive repairs.

By 1962 the control of railway workshops had been transferred from the CM&EE to the newly introduced Workshops Division of British Railways who promptly conducted a complete survey of locomotive workshops. With the run down of the steam locomotive fleet and the lower requirements for diesel locomotive maintenance, they discovered there was an excess of workshop capacity. Accordingly the decision was taken to run down Stratford Works with final closure occurring in September 1963. However, the CM&EE department of the Eastern Region was unhappy that locomotives requiring unclassified repairs had to take their turn with all other locomotives requiring attention at the main workshops. From this came the idea of reopening the ERS as Regional Repair Shops changing their name to the Diesel Repair Shop or DRS.

This was the beginning of an interesting period for the works, a great variety of jobs being undertaken by the workforce. In 1978 work was done on the power cars for High Speed Trains used on the East Coast route. Modification in conjunction with engineers from the power unit manufacturers included the fitting of an exhaust deflector to the roof. Also at this time the DRS undertook a series of modifications on the Rumanian built Class 56 locomotives. These involved replacing the bogies with a pair that had been refurbished by a contractor in Wolverhampton in addition to re-routing traction motor conduits and fitting new traction motor junction boxes.

By the early 1980s many of the first generation diesel locomotives were approaching the end of their working lives and a policy of cannibalising the various classes was introduced. Involved in this exercise were the types `40´, `45´, `46´, `25´ and `Deltic´ Class 55s. The main components to be exchanged were the power units and bogies and in the case of the Class 55s the nameplates had to be removed from the scrap locomotives. In addition to this work in the early 1980s was a contract to construct six snowploughs from redundant Class 40 bogies, the snowplough blades being built by Beilhack in Germany.

The first warning that all was not well at DRS came in January 1990 when they lost the work of Class 86/2 bogie overhauls to BREL Crewe and in April 1990 they lost the Class 87 programme to Springburn Level 5 Depot in Glasgow. In October 1990 final closure of Stratford works was announced as there was over-capacity in the Level 5 Group, the works closing on 31 March 1991.

Above:
Outshopped from Stratford Works after a General repair some two weeks earlier on 25 July 1958, Stratford (30A) MPD´s Class B1 4-6-0 No 61135 is seen on shed. This allocation was short-lived as was its next transfer to Parkeston (30F) MPD. Subsequent allocation to Doncaster in October 1959 was to be its final move. *R.C. Riley*

Below:
Always kept in `Ex-Works´ condition were the Liverpool St station pilots. Here, Class N7/3 No 69614, its Westinghouse air-pump steaming wildly, is depicted at the station on 14 March 1959. In the background, Norwich (32A) MPD´s `Britannia´ No 70039 *Sir Christopher Wren,* **awaits departure with `The Norfolkman´.** *T.B. Owen*

Above:
Class J20 0-6-0 No 64690 is seen outside Stratford MPD on 7 June 1959 following a General repair at the Works. It is carrying the new BR `Lion & Wheel´ emblem. *R.C. Riley*

Below:
Withdrawn from traffic in October 1958, Cambridge (31A) MPD's Class D16/3 4-4-0 No 62588 awaits cutting up at Stratford Works on 2 May 1959. This variation of the class, introduced in 1933, was a rebuild of the 'D15' class with a larger boiler, round-topped firebox and modified footplate. *Colour-Rail*